INVENTORY 98

INVENTORY 1985

THE LAW OF THE ANCIENT ROMANS

THE LAW OF
THE ANCIENT ROMANS

ALAN WATSON

SOUTHERN METHODIST UNIVERSITY PRESS • DALLAS

For John Barton and Robin Seager

CONTENTS

PREFACE

This is an attempt to synthesize Roman law and explain its development from the foundation of the city, traditionally in 753 B.C., to the time of the Emperor Justinian in the sixth century A.D. Its system of private law was Rome's greatest gift to the world but is, ironically, often thought too technical and remote for the comprehension of the man in the street, the practical lawyer and even the classical scholar. Yet it is basically very simple—otherwise it would not have transplanted to other civilizations so easily. Roman society was itself much simpler than modern western society and it did not need the legal technicalities which beset our lives. For convenience the Latin legal terms and the names of actions are usually given in this book but very few of them need to be remembered for an understanding of the subject. The means by which the law developed is stressed to show its extraordinary vitality and the Roman genius for legal thought. For the same reasons particular details have been given prominence. Criminal law was not of the same compelling interest to the Romans and has had little influence: it is outside the scope of this book.

Disputes rage among scholars on many rules of Roman law. In general the view I have expressed is my own, even where it is not shared by the majority.

ALAN WATSON

THE LAW OF THE ANCIENT ROMANS

I

LAW AND THE ROMAN MIND

ROME'S GREATEST LEGACY to the modern world is undoubtedly its private law. Roman law forms the basis of all the legal systems of Western Europe with the exception of England (but not of Scotland) and Scandinavia. Outside Europe, the law of places so diverse as Louisiana and Ceylon, Quebec and Japan, Abyssinia and South Africa is based firmly on Roman law. Even in England and the countries of Anglo-American law in general, the influence of Roman law is considerable and is much greater than is often admitted.

The excellence and influence of Roman law are due to three main factors. First, the Romans took an abiding interest in law and the courts, which I will look at more closely in this chapter. Second, they developed a system in which change was relatively easy and the power to make important reforms was in the hands of the best legal minds. The sources of law will be specifically discussed in the third chapter, and this flexibility of the law will continually emerge as we go along. Third, the Emperor Justinian's codification of the law in the sixth century A.D. gave later lawyers a short but comprehensive account of a highly developed legal system which made an easy model to copy. Consideration of this is postponed until the tenth chapter.

The Romans' interest in law and the courts can be traced back to the earliest days. The traditional date for the foundation of Rome is 753 B.C., and the emergent city was ruled by kings until the expulsion of Tarquin the Proud in 509 B.C. The ancient sources have it that the kings were responsible for a surprisingly large amount of legislation, especially in the fields of sacred and family law.

According to Dionysius of Halicarnassus, the founder of Rome, Romulus, allowed each of the common people (the plebeians) to choose a patron from the patricians, and rights and duties were assigned to both patricians and plebeians.[1] The patrons' duties were "to interpret the law

1. 2.9f.

3

for their clients, to bring law suits for them if they suffered injury, and to assist them when they were bringing an action." These are the only duties mentioned for the patricians. Little early Latin literature has come down to us, but in the first writer of whose work much has survived we find the same emphasis on law and litigation. Plautus, the comic play-wright who flourished around the end of the third and beginning of the second century B.C., makes a drunk man say in his play, *Mostellaria:* "Now I want to tell you why you should think that men are like houses. First of all, parents are the builders of their children. They lay their foundations, they build them up, they do their best to construct them soundly. They spare no material to make them useful and handsome both for the public and for themselves. They polish them, teach them letters, the principles of general law and statute law, they expend their money and labour that others may pray that their own sons be like them. . . . They leave the builders' hands. . . . Up to that point, while I was in the hands of the constructors I was a good clean-living chap. But when I gained my independence I ruined the builders' work, at once and com-pletely."[2] The knowledge of law is here emphasized as the outstanding mark of a fine man. This knowledge included both statute law–that is, state-enacted law–and general juristic law–that is, law as it was devel-oped by legal writers. Both kinds are expressly mentioned by Plautus, and it is significant that he names no other kind of practical skill. In another play, *Casina,*[3] Plautus introduces the duty of appearing in court for an acquaintance. A lover complains about spending his time in court when he could have been enjoying himself with his girlfriend: "In my opinion it is completely silly for any man to have to set out for the forum the day that his girl friend was all ready for him–just as I did, fool that I am. I wasted the day, acting as advocate for some relative of mine. He lost his case and, by Hercules, I am glad of it, I certainly am for asking me away to appear for him today, to no purpose. In my opinion a man who asks others to appear for him in court ought to question them first to find out whether his advocate has got his wits about him or not." The implication of the Latin is that the relative he represented in court was not very close. And it is made plain that to appear for someone in court was a serious duty which could not lightly be refused, and had to be given precedence over mere pleasure.

Terence, writing slightly later, describes a meeting of a young man, Chaerea, with an elderly relative: "Immediately he rushes up to me from

2. 118ff.
3. 563ff.

a great distance, bent, shaking, with hanging jaw, groaning. 'Hey, Chaerea,' he said. I stopped. 'Do you know what I wanted to say to you?' 'Tell me.' 'I have a legal suit tomorrow.' 'So what?' 'I want you to tell your father to remember to appear for me in court early.' While he was saying this an hour went by."[4]

The clearest indication, though, of the social importance which a knowledge of law had for the early Romans is in Cicero. At the beginning of his work, *The Ends of Good and Evil*, Cicero attempts to justify the study of philosophy. One of his observations is that law–which he regards as a far less important discipline than philosophy–is widely regarded as a proper study for the leaders of the state. The politicians discuss even the most minor points of law. "There was a discussion," he says, "between the leading men of the state, Publius Scaevola and Manius Manilius as to whether the child of a slave girl belonged to the mother's owner when the owner had given someone else the right to the use and fruits of the slave. Marcus Brutus disagreed with them."[5] A petty point of law indeed, but the men who were devoting their time to discussing it were important men of the second century B.C. Scaevola was consul–the consulship was the highest public office–in 133 B.C., Manilius was consul in 149 B.C., and Brutus was praetor–the praetorship was the second most important office–in 142 B.C.

This passion for law and its application led to a swift realization of the nature of law, and therefore to the separation of law and morality and of law and religion to a degree unequaled in the ancient world. The separation of law and morality means that in an individual case the decision should be reached on the basis of legal principle and not on what is fair in the particular circumstances. Cicero could say, "Injustice also often arises through trickery and by an over-subtle but wicked interpretation of the law. Accordingly the phrase 'The stricter the law, the greater the injustice' has now become a common saying."[6] And one of Terence's characters quotes "The strictest law is often the greatest wickedness."[7]

An example of this separation of law and morality can be seen in connection with the stipulation *(stipulatio)*. This was a formal verbal contract, known at least as early as the fifth century B.C., which was valid because of the form of words used. The form alone was important, and whether the contract was induced by fraud or fear was totally

4. *Eunuchus* 335ff.
5. *De finibus* 4.12.
6. *De officiis* 1.10.33.
7. *Heautontimorumenos* 796.

irrelevant. No remedies were available to the innocent victim of extortion in such a situation until about 80 B.C., and only in 66 B.C. was protection against fraud introduced. This distinction between law and morality, once made, in turn accelerates the development of a rational and almost scientific system of law.

That the Romans drew a clear distinction between law and morality naturally does not mean that their law was unaffected by ideas of what constituted moral behavior. Thus, it seems that in early law divorce was permitted only for specific matrimonial offenses. Again, in early times breach of promise of marriage gave rise to a legal action, but a change in social attitudes resulted in the disappearance of the action, probably before the end of the third century B.C. In the Empire, too, there was considerable legislation to protect slaves from cruel masters. And the praetors, who had control over lawsuits, could decide to allow a suit to proceed when no legal action had previously been provided, and they could refuse permission for an action to be brought even where an action was provided by law. An instance of the latter type can be dated to 70 B.C.[8] In 74 B.C. a praetor refused to give possession of an inheritance to the heir named in the will–though by his own proclamation (edict)[9] he had declared that he would give possession to the testamentary heir–because the heir was a brothel-keeper and the praetor "thought that the position of a brothel and the forum should be kept separate."[10] What is important is that the Romans accepted the principle that the concept of law was different from the idea of morality, though frequently affected by it.

Religion and law were also kept apart. Religious sanctions were one thing, legal sanctions another. It is true, though, that much of the legislation of the kings, as it is reported to us, is concerned with the ordering of religious rites. It is also true that the pontiffs, the leaders of the state religion, had until well into the Republic very considerable control over the forms of legal action. But this second matter, looked at more closely, demonstrates best of all the separation of law and religion. The office of pontifex maximus (high priest) was elective and was a reward for public service. It was not a full-time post, and the occupant did not dedicate his whole life to divine service. Thus, Julius Caesar was elected pontifex maximus in 63 B.C., after heavy bribery. But there is nowhere the slightest indication that any of the pontiffs ever attempted to use their power over judicial proceedings for the aggrandizement of the state religion, or

8. Valerius Maximus 7.7.5.
9. For the praetor's Edict, see below, pp. 21ff.
10. Valerius Maximus 7.7.7.

to introduce religious ideas into the law. Indeed the reverse is sometimes true. The same famous jurist, Publius Mucius Scaevola, who has already been mentioned, was pontifex maximus, yet it was he who developed or advised a dodge whereby a person who was left property by will could take it without performing the obligatory family rites of the deceased.[11] This separation of law and religion continued even after the Empire became Christian. Despite the church fathers' repeated condemnations of divorce, and the acceptance of the invalidity of divorce by the early Christian churches, divorce without formalities and at the request of either spouse was still legally valid–though under penalty–up to and including the time of the Emperor Justinian in the sixth century A.D.

The Romans' delight in law and the courts can be at least partly explained by social conditions. The great cleavage between the upper and lower classes, especially after slavery became common, meant that labor and paid employment were openly disdained. Few activities were therefore available to the active rich, and these were all concerned with public service. Just as in Athens many of the best minds turned to philosophy, so the more practical Romans turned to law. The other two permissible forms of "work" were a military career and politics, and in fact the three were inextricably linked in the lives of many prominent Romans. To be elected to public office it was helpful to have a distinguished army career or a reputation for advocacy, or indeed both. Javolenus Priscus, a distinguished jurist of the first century A.D., commanded several legions, held the consulship, and was successively governor of Upper Germany, Syria, and Africa. Cicero, a man of no family connections, was able to climb to the top of the political ladder because of the reputation he built up in the courts as an orator. Moreover, just as political officeholders were unpaid, so it was laid down that payment could not be exacted for an advocate's or jurist's services. In theory at least, an advocate was forbidden even to accept gifts from a grateful client.

Public recognition might seem to favor oratory rather than the development of legal science, but oratory had to have its basis in a knowledge of the law. And the Roman social custom whereby every rich man was surrounded by a circle of poor dependants, with reciprocal rights and duties, inevitably placed on the rich the task of being able to give legal advice. The early control of the forms of process by the pontiffs–with the power this would give to modify law–and the right of the higher magistrates, especially the praetors and the curule aediles, to issue Edicts changing the effect of the law, also meant that there was during the whole

11. Cicero, *De legibus* 2.21.53.

of the Republic a considerable body of influential persons who were largely concerned with legal improvement. Their willingness to make improvements, of course, always assumes that there was in any event wide public interest in private law. But this we know to be the case. Again I can refer to the comic playwright Plautus, who was not writing for the educated public but had to compete with bear-baiting for his audience. His plays are full of legal jokes and elaborate legal scenes; he makes puns on the forms of pawning property;[12] parodies the aediles' Edict;[13] carefully explains in a prologue that though his play will deal with the marriage of slaves which was not possible at Rome, such marriages were valid elsewhere and especially where his play was set;[14] shows a character framing the conditions of a fraudulent sale in such a way that the buyer will have no remedy;[15] correctly–according to comic tradition– uses technical terms for aggravated theft *(furtum manifestum)*;[16] and so on.

What part was played in all this by the characteristics of the Roman race cannot easily be determined. Obviously the Roman temperament cannot be irrelevant to the Roman passion for law. Yet once Rome had spread its boundaries beyond Italy, Roman citizens of non-Italic stock were also prominent among the jurists.

This juristic activity meant that the law became extremely detailed and that fine distinctions were continually being drawn. Two texts concerned with damage to property will illustrate this:

> If you kill my slave, I think personal feelings are not to be evaluated in money terms, for example if someone kills your natural son (i.e., born to someone else's slave girl) whom you would have bought for a high price, but only for what he would be worth on the open market. Sextius Pedius also says that the price of things is to be estimated not according to the feelings or values of individuals, but in a general way. And so a person who has possession of his natural son is not richer because he would have bought him back for a high sum if another had possessed him; nor has a person who possesses another's son as much money as he could have sold him for to his father.[17]

> If someone hired a slave to drive a mule and the mule was entrusted to him, and the slave tied the mule by its halter to his thumb whereafter the mule rushed off in such a way that it tore off the slave's thumb and dashed itself from a height,

---

12. *Epidicus* 697ff.
13. *Captivi* 802ff.
14. *Casina* 68ff.
15. *Persa* 135ff., 329ff., 524f., 577ff., 665, 714f.
16. *Poenulus* 711-785.
17. *Digest of Justinian* 9.2.33 pr. (Paul).

Mela writes that if an unskilled slave were hired out as skilled, an action can be brought on the contract of hire against the slave's owner on account of the injured mule; but if the mule was agitated by someone striking or frightening it, then the owner of the mule and the owner of the slave will have an action under the Aquilian law *(lex Aquilia)* against the person who upset it. I think that in the situation where there is an action under the contract of hire, there is also an action under the Aquilian law.[18]

Even as early as the second century B.C., Manilius had written a book on, or made a collection of, the different clauses which could be used in a contract of sale.[19]

18. *Digest of Justinian* 9.2.27.3 (Ulpian).
19. Cicero *De oratore* 1.58.246; Varro *De re rustica* 2.3.5, 2.5.11, 2.7.6.

II

THE LAWS OF THE KINGS AND
THE TWELVE TABLES

ROME, THE TRADITION GOES, was founded by Romulus in 753 B.C., and, until the expulsion of Tarquin the Proud in 509 B.C., was ruled successively by seven kings. Our sources credit these monarchs with a surprisingly large amount of legislation, which was apparently mainly, but not exclusively, concerned with sacred and family law.[1] Modern scholars usually deny the existence of such legislation. They claim that legislation at so early a date is most implausible, that the Roman writers fell into the fallacy of thinking that there can be no law without legislation, and that these collections of so-called laws are in any event not early. But these arguments may be overlooking the Roman capacity for law and its organization. Whether these provisions preserved to us should actually count as legislation or not, it is reasonable to believe that they do give us a tolerably accurate picture of law in the regal period. To begin with, the provisions taken together–and they come from a number of sources though primarily from Plutarch and the antiquarian Dionysius of Halicarnassus–form a harmonious system, and this is something one would not expect from mere later invention, especially since the provisions are recounted with no obvious general tendency towards praise or blame. This system does not correspond to the law of any later period in Rome, and is in marked contrast to the law of the Twelve Tables (which date from the middle of the fifth century B.C.) and of the time of Plutarch and Dionysius themselves. So one cannot simply believe that the Romans attributed later rules to a much earlier period. At the same time, no other system of law known to us could have supplied the model which the writers took to be early Roman. Finally there are enough similarities between these provisions and later Roman law to suggest that the former is the ultimate source of the latter.

I can illustrate these arguments by looking at the position of the head

1. The sources will be found collected in *Fontes iuris romani antejustiniani,* vol. 1, *Leges,* 2nd edit. (Florence, 1941), pp. 4ff.

of a family (the paterfamilias), which is the aspect of private law most fully documented for the regal period. The paterfamilias had enormous powers over his wife and his descendants, but to judge from the sources these powers were more restricted then than they were later. Romulus laid down, we are told,[2] that a Roman citizen had to bring up all his male children and his first-born daughter and could not kill any of his children under the age of three, though malformed babies or monsters could be exposed immediately after birth provided they were first shown to five near neighbors who approved or attested this. Later, as early as the Twelve Tables, all these restrictions had gone, and the paterfamilias could expose all his infants without check. In more developed Roman law the paterfamilias had complete power over all his children even when fully grown and could kill them or sell them into slavery. These rights were also said to have been first granted by Romulus.[3] But a law of Numa, the second king, denied the father's right to sell a son whom he had permitted to marry.[4] This restriction on the father's power also no longer existed in the law of a later period. Romulus decreed that a husband could divorce his wife only for poisoning offspring (abortion?), adultery, or tampering with the keys (attempted adultery?). If he sent her away otherwise, half of his property went to his wife, the other half was given to the goddess Ceres.[5] By the later Republic no grounds were necessary for divorce, and the sole penalty for unjustified divorce concerned the retention or return of the wife's dowry. If the wife committed adultery or drank wine, Romulus ruled that she could be killed on the instructions of her family council with the consent of her husband.[6] Later the husband had an unfettered legal right to kill his wife whether she had misbehaved or not, and her family had no say in the matter. From these provisions reported for the regal period it would seem that the powers of the paterfamilias were restricted and that they were greater a short time later. This pattern of development is exactly the reverse of what would be expected by anyone not experienced in anthropology and would not have been invented by the later Romans. It thus provides strong evidence that the picture we have of the substance of Roman law under the kings is generally correct.

We have some information on other aspects of private law in the regal period. Romulus enacted that each of the plebeians had to choose a

2. By Dionysius, 2.15.
3. Dionysius 2.26.27.
4. Dionysius 2.27.
5. Plutarch *Romulus* 22.
6. Dionysius 2.25.6.

patron from the patricians.[7] The patricians had to interpret law for their
clients, bring lawsuits for them if they suffered injury, and assist them
when they were bringing a legal action. The clients were to help their
patron find dowries for his daughters if he was short of money, pay the
ransom if the patron or his sons were captured by an enemy, and pay
the damages or fine if he lost a civil or criminal action. Neither patron
nor client could accuse or give evidence against the other or cast a vote
against him; the penalty for breach was death.[8] Romulus also enacted
that a wife could not divorce her husband[9] and–important for later
development[10]–that if a father sold his son three times the son would
become completely free from his father's power.[11] A number of laws are
attributed to Numa, the second king. He ordered each person to mark
clearly the boundaries of his land,[12] established that the willful killing of
any free man was murder,[13] and laid down a relatively light penalty for
negligent killing.[14] He further enacted that if a pregnant woman died she
was not to be buried before the fetus was cut out of her,[15] to give it a
chance of life. For a primitive society–as Rome then was–these provisions are quite remarkable. The sixth king, Servius Tullius, was responsible for the rule, unique in the ancient world for its liberality, that slaves
who were freed were to become Roman citizens. This rule was never
basically changed at Rome. He also separated public trials from private
lawsuits.

The Roman aptitude for law is thus early revealed, but the true
Roman genius first appears in their earliest codification of law, the
Twelve Tables. This was regarded by the Romans themselves as the basic
foundation of all their law,[16] and in Cicero's time school children learned
it by heart.[17]

The story of the codification according to the sources is this. In the
first half of the fifth century B.C., as at other times, there were difficulties
between the patricians and the plebeians. Part of the plebeians' grievance
was that they did not know what the law was since this was, in effect,

7. Dionysius 2.9.
8. Dionysius 2.10.
9. Plutarch *Romulus* 22.
10. See below, pp. 37ff.
11. Dionysius 2.26.27.
12. Dionysius 2.74.
13. Festus, s.v. *Parricidii.*
14. Servius *Commentarii in Vergili Eclogas* 4.43.
15. *Digest of Justinian* 11.8.2.
16. Cf. Livy 3.34.6.
17. Cicero *De legibus* 2.4.9.

a secret preserve of the pontiffs, and that the judges did not regard themselves as bound by the law. So in 462 B.C., a tribune of the plebs, Gaius Terentilius Harsa, proposed that a commission of five men should be established to draw up a code of laws which would be binding upon the consuls–the holders of the highest political office–in the exercise of their judicial powers. For it was in name only, he said, that the authority of the consuls was less hateful than that of kings; in reality it was almost worse "since we have accepted two masters instead of one, who have infinite and uncontrolled power and who, unbridled and free from all restraint themselves, turn the fear of the law and all tortures on the common people."[18] For eight years, the patricians successfully resisted the proposal, but eventually they had to give in. Still, to gain a further delay they sent an embassy to Greece to study the code of Solon, the famous Athenian lawgiver. This Attic code is traditionally dated 594-593 B.C. When the embassy returned, the ordinary constitution was temporarily suspended, and ten men (decemviri) were elected as the chief magistrates. Plebeians were eligible for election as well as patricians, but actually only patricians were chosen. In 451 B.C. the decemviri produced their code, which was written on ten bronze tablets and placed in the market place. The decemviri, whose fairmindedness is stressed, asked the people to read the tablets, to consider each individual point and discuss it among themselves, and to declare publicly the faults of the codification. After amendment, the law of the Ten Tables was formally adopted, but it came to be felt that the codification required two further tablets. Elections for a further commission of ten men for the following year were held; there was much canvassing, and this time some plebeians were elected.[19] These decemviri turned tyrannous and wanted to hold power indefinitely but after a secession of the plebs they were thrown out. Nonetheless, the decemviri had produced the further two tables, and though these were unjust they were formally accepted.[20] Thus runs the Roman account of the formation of the Twelve Tables.

The story, however, is unlikely to be completely accurate. The idea of an embassy to Athens is most implausible. There is no trace of the embassy in any of the Greek sources, and Rome at that time could scarcely have had much knowledge of or contact with other Mediterranean states outside Italy. A few modern scholars have even suggested that 451 B.C. is far too early for the codification and have proposed to date it around 300 or even 200 B.C. This view is rightly rejected, both

18. Livy 3.9.1ff.
19. Livy 3.35.
20. Livy 3.36.

because historical activities for these later periods are well known and it is inconceivable that the Romans of Cicero's time could have been taken in by a relatively recent fabrication, and because the law of the Twelve Tables is much more archaic in spirit than could be expected for even 300 B.C. Moreover, if a late date is postulated for the Twelve Tables it is difficult to see how the flexible system of Cicero's day would have had time to develop.

Naturally, the original bronze tablets have not survived and the contents of the Twelve Tables have to be reconstructed from odd scraps of evidence.[21] These scraps do not provide us with the complete code, but since the Twelve Tables were regarded as so fundamental it is likely that we have some knowledge of all the more important provisions. And we can deduce quite a lot about the general character of the code. Above all, unlike modern codifications it is not comprehensive, but, like other early codes, it tends to deal with the less ordinary situation and to ignore the straightforward ones. Thus, we have provisions about what is to happen if a son does damage or if a slave does damage and even one about the legal results when an animal causes harm. But we have nothing about the ordinary case where the head of the household does damage. It is implausible to suggest that the relevant clause has been lost, for the same thing occurs in other early codes such as the great Jewish codification, the Mishpatim. That has particular clauses on damage caused by my cattle or by a pit I have dug or by a fire I made in my field, but none on the case when I directly caused the damage. Again, in the Twelve Tables mancipation *(mancipatio)*, the formal mode of transfer of certain kinds of important things, is simply declared to be valid, but the requirements for its form are not discussed. The explanation of all this is that the plain straightforward case could be taken for granted.

Full details of the rules of the Twelve Tables will not be given here since the main ones will emerge in later chapters, but enough will be said to illustrate the extent of legal development. Procedure is extensively considered in the code, and the idea of someone appearing on behalf of the plaintiff or defendant is well established. It was he who bound himself financially for the appearance of his "client" in court on the due day. In one form of action the plaintiff and the defendant each swore an oath that his own case was just, and whoever lost the action had to pay the amount of the oath, five hundred *asses* (an *as* was a monetary unit of copper) if the matter at issue concerned more than a thousand *asses*, fifty *asses* if the matter concerned less than a thousand. Where the action concerned

21. These scraps will be found collected in *Fontes*, vol. 1, pp. 26ff.

a man's liberty, the oath was always for fifty no matter how valuable the man would be if it was proved that he was a slave. Provision was made for the appointment of guardians to those who were regarded as unable to look after their own affairs–women, infants, lunatics, and prodigals. In the case of transfer of ownership by *mancipatio* there was an automatic guarantee that if the recipient were evicted, the transferor would pay him double the amount of the price stated in the *mancipatio*. But this built-in guarantee came into operation only if the price were paid or security given for payment. The making of a will was recognized as a man's normal right. When under a will a slave was to become free on paying a certain sum of money to the heir, if before he did so the heir sold him he would get his freedom on paying the purchaser the amount mentioned in the will. An action was given to settle disputes over boundaries, and another to protect a person whose land was in danger from flooding as a result of work done on a neighbor's property. A man could collect acorns (used for feeding pigs) which fell from his trees onto a neighbor's land and could lop off up to fifteen feet from the ground the branches of a neighbor's tree which overhung his land. A fixed scale of financial compensation was laid down for most physical injuries. When a limb was actually destroyed, the injured party could wreak the same vengeance on the wrongdoer, but the wording of the text indicates that this rule was only to come into operation if the parties could not agree upon proper financial compensation. Perhaps most surprising of all, the Twelve Tables recognized the existence of a form cf contract, though contract is normally a branch of law which is extremely slow to develop. This contract was the stipulation *(stipulatio)*. The formalities were that the contract was created by a spoken question followed immediately by a spoken answer; hence the parties had to be face to face. One party asked, "Do you promise on your oath?" *(spondesne?)*; the other replied, "I promise on my oath" *(spondeo)*. The contract was construed according to strict law, and only what was actually said was relevant for the interpretation of the contract. With its limitations the stipulation is nonetheless a remarkable achievement.

Some of the provisions may appear gruesome to modern eyes. For example, if after the performance of various legal rites and the passage of a certain amount of time–all carefully defined–a debtor had still not paid his creditors, they could divide his body among them. In contrast to the law portrayed in Shakespeare's *The Merchant of Venice*, the Twelve Tables' clause expressly and wisely states that the creditors will be free from liability if they cut too much or too little.

The style of the Twelve Tables is impressive. It is marked by great brevity, clarity, and simplicity, which indicates that the draftsmen must have been men of experience with a long tradition of law behind them. Even if we accept the idea that an embassy was sent to Athens to study the laws of Solon, the influence of Attic law is slight. Gaius, a jurist of the second century A.D. who wrote a commentary on the Twelve Tables, says that the provision that members of a club or society may make their own rules if these do not contravene the law of the land is taken from the laws of Solon;[22] and elsewhere he claims that the clause dealing with activities such as the planting of trees at the edge of one's land is modeled on the laws of Solon.[23] For the rest, what we have seems to be native Roman, and this is in harmony with the idea that what the plebeians wanted was to be able to know the law, not to reform it.

22. *Digest of Justinian* 47.22.4.
23. *Digest of Justinian* 10.1.13.

III

THE SOURCES OF LAW

ROMAN LAW WAS exceptionally fortunate in its contemporary elementary textbooks. One was written by an obscure jurist called Gaius around the middle of the second century A.D. Little is known about Gaius, not even the rest of his name or whether he was Roman or provincial. No reference to him by a contemporary jurist has come down to us. But his *Institutes* eventually became the standard textbook throughout the Empire, in the Greek East and Egypt as well as in the West. It is not a coincidence that this is the only work from the classical period (the first 250 years of the Empire) which has survived virtually complete. Although we have only one full manuscript and that a palimpsest,[1] more fragments of the *Institutes* have turned up than of any other classical juristic writing. The manuscript which we have was written in the fifth or sixth century A.D., which illustrates how long the book remained popular and is some indication of its high quality. In 533 A.D. the Emperor Justinian issued his *Institutes,* which were mainly modeled on Gaius's though the law was brought up to date. Justinian's *Institutes,* though meant as a textbook for first-year law students, were issued as an imperial statute. Accordingly, the Roman elementary textbooks, as we know them, are peculiarly authoritative: Gaius's *Institutes* for their quality and influence on Roman legal teaching; Justinian's *Institutes* in addition because they were themselves the law of the land. In this and the succeeding chapters there will be continued reliance on the *Institutes* of Gaius and of Justinian.

Justinian tells us that Roman law is either written or unwritten.[2] Written law is statute, plebiscites, decrees of the senate *(senatuscon-sulta),* the decisions of the emperors, and the replies of the jurists. Unwritten law is that which usage has approved, "for everyday customs,

1. That is, the original writing has been scraped or washed off (and can be read only with difficulty) so that the parchment can be used again. In this case Gaius's *Institutes* were replaced by the writings of Saint Jerome.

2. *Institutes of Justinian* 1.2.3.

which are approved by the users, imitate statute."[3] Thus, the distinction between written and unwritten law is the literal one and is free from the traditional Anglo-American ambiguity. All law which is written down is written law; law which is not written down is unwritten law. The only law which is not written down is, of course, custom. Gaius in his enumeration of the sources of law does not mention unwritten law. The fact is–and it is of considerable significance–that custom as a source of new law was very unimportant.

Of course, if one goes back to the beginning, one will find that most of the fundamental rules derive from custom. For instance, custom will determine what formalities are required for the forms of transfer of ownership even though these forms may later be given statutory approval. Indeed, the very lawmaking power of the state must ultimately be based on customary acceptance of the state's authority. But once the early days are past, the question whether custom can make new law is very different. In the Republic there are very few cases of custom making law, and in fact only one certain case. The Twelve Tables laid down that if a man bought a beast for a sacrificial offering but failed to pay for it, the seller could seize some of the buyer's property as security for payment provided he uttered certain formal words as he did so. The same rule applied when a person who wanted money for a sacrificial feast hired out an animal to someone who failed to pay. The censors later applied this procedure also against persons who, under a statute, owed taxes to tax farmers. So far custom does not come into it. But by custom this procedure was extended in certain cases for the benefit of soldiers. If a soldier did not receive his pay he could act in this way against the person who was supposed to pay him. Similarly if he were granted money with which to buy his horse and the money was not given him, and the same is true of money granted for the purchase of barley for his horse.[4] But there is no sign of any theory of custom in the Republic. Questions such as how long must a custom be observed before it becomes law, or which is to prevail in a conflict between statute and custom, remain unasked, far less answered. For the Empire there is a statement of the jurist Julian, preserved for us in Justinian's *Digest:* "Age-long custom is properly regarded as law. . . . Since even statutes bind us only because they have been accepted by the judgement of the people, it is right that what the people has approved without any writing should be binding upon all. For what does it matter whether the people declares its wishes by vote or by

3. *Institutes of Justinian* 1.2.9.
4. Gaius *Institutes* 4.26-29.

actual conduct?"[5] Despite this and despite the agonized searches of modern scholars no clear case has been produced where custom made law at Rome–as opposed to provincial practice–in the Empire. The Emperor Constantine declared in 319 A.D., "The authority of custom and long usage is not slight but not to the extent that it will prevail against reason or against a statute."[6] The significance of the unimportance of custom is twofold. First, it demonstrates the richness of written Roman law–there was no scope for custom to play an important role. Second, it means that the sources of law are much more under the control of the authorities. Political factors are indeed prominent in the sources of written law, and for this reason there is a great deal of difference between the sources in the Republic and the sources in the Empire.

SOURCES OF WRITTEN LAW IN THE REPUBLIC

Statutes were passed by an assembly *(comitia)* of the people, whether the *comitia centuriata* or the *comitia tributa*. The *comitia centuriata* was the people assembled in military order, but in historical times the military aspect had ceased to be important. For this assembly in the years before 241 B.C., the people were divided according to wealth into five classes and each class was divided into centuries. The first class, the wealthiest and also numerically the smallest, had 80 centuries; the second, third, and fourth had 20 centuries each; and the fifth had 30 centuries. In addition to these there were 18 centuries for the knights *(equites)* –and knighthood was based on a wealth qualification – 4 centuries for artificers and buglers, and finally 1 century for the *proletarii,* those who had not the necessary financial qualification for even the lowest class. Voting was by centuries, not by individuals, and there were 193 centuries. The first class with the support of the *equites* could muster 98 votes and so could always outvote the others. Between 241 and 218 B.C. this *comitia* was reformed, but its marked bias in favor of wealth remained. The main work of the *comitia centuriata* was the election of magistrates. The other important *comitia,* the *comitia tributa,* was based on the old division into tribes, which was originally territorial. Our knowledge of the *comitia tributa* and what it did is rather scanty. It certainly existed as early as the Twelve Tables, but it tends to be confused in the sources with the assembly of the people *(concilium plebis)* which was also organized into tribes.

5. *Digest of Justinian* 1.3.32.
6. *Code of Justinian* 8.52 (53).2.

The early history of the *concilium plebis* is unclear, but as early as 471 B.C.[7] it was enacted that its arrangement should be by tribes, and so it remained. As will be readily imagined, this body was prominent in the continued class war between the patricians and the plebeians. The enactments *(plebiscita)* of the *concilium* were not strictly statutes at first and were binding only on the plebeians. But we are told of three separate statutes, of 449, 339, and 287 B.C., which enacted that plebiscites should have the force of law and be binding on all the people. The legal sources mention only the last statute, the *lex Hortensia* of 287, and it is quite likely that this was in fact the only one.

These three bodies then, *comitia centuriata, comitia tributa,* and *concilium plebis,* could legislate. Which body did legislate in a particular instance depended upon the magistrate who wished to have a proposal accepted by the people. A Roman assembly could meet only when summoned by a magistrate; the *comitia centuriata* was normally under the presidency of a consul, the *comitia tributa* had to be summoned by a "patrician" magistrate, that is, one elected by all the people, and the *concilium plebis* by a magistrate of the plebs. The assembly could deal only with matters brought before it by the magistrate, there was no discussion or opportunity for amendment, and all that the assembly could do was accept or reject the magistrate's bill. In practice, though, the bill was usually first debated in the very aristocratic senate, which throughout the Republic had itself no lawmaking powers. In the circumstances it is perhaps not surprising that most legislation was political and that there are in fact few statutes concerned with private law. Even in some of those a political motive is not hard to find. This applies to the number passed to protect the guarantor of a debt–persons liable to pay a debt always seem more numerous than creditors. Still, some statutes brought considerable advances in the civil law. The *lex Canuleia* of 445 B.C. allowed patricians and plebeians to intermarry; the *lex Atilia* of about 210 B.C. provided for the appointment by the praetor and a majority of the tribunes of the plebs of a tutor to a fatherless child who otherwise would have no guardian; the *lex Cincia* of 204 B.C. restricted large gifts; the *lex Plaetoria* of 193/192 B.C. gave remedies when a person under twenty-five was defrauded; the *lex Atinia* of around 150 B.C. laid down that no one could become the owner of stolen property until it had returned into the hands of the person from whom it was stolen; and important procedural reforms–what these were is uncertain–were introduced by the *lex Aebutia* in the second half of the second century B.C.

7. Livy 2.58.1.

Most important of all was the *lex Aquilia,* which probably went through several stages of development before the final one of 287 B.C. and which regulated virtually all the law of damage to property. There are indications that the *concilium plebis* was the most active assembly for private law legislation; the *lex Aquilia* was a plebiscite.[8]

A Roman classification divides statutes into imperfect laws, less than perfect laws, and perfect laws. An imperfect law is one which forbids an act but neither declares it void if it is performed nor imposes a penalty. A less than perfect law forbids an act and, though it does not declare the act void if it is performed, it does impose a penalty. A perfect law prohibits an act and declares it invalid if it is performed. The first two types are common in the Republic, but not the last, which apparently does not appear at all. In the Empire, on the other hand, perfect laws are very common. Modern scholars have advanced a number of hypotheses for the popularity of imperfect and less than perfect statutes in the Republic, but none of these is particularly plausible.

All in all it was probably very fortunate that in the Republic statutes played a restricted part in the development of law. Of fundamental importance, though, were the Edicts of the magistrates. All the higher magistrates had power to issue Edicts within their own sphere of competence. For us the most important are those of the urban praetor and the peregrine praetor, and to a lesser, though still considerable, extent that of the curule aediles.

It became the custom for the praetor–the magistrate immediately below consul in rank–when he entered upon his office to put up a conspicuous notice in the forum saying how he was going to enforce the law. It is not known how soon this development began but Plautus, writing around the beginning of the second century B.C., makes at least one joke about a particular edict.[9] Technically the praetor could not change the law, but he had control of the law courts, and he could lay down in his Edict that in circumstances when the civil law gave an action he would refuse to allow it to be brought and, conversely, when the civil law gave no action he would give a remedy. Each praetor held office for a year and his Edict was valid only while he was in office, but inevitably it came about that an ever-growing number of clauses were automatically renewed each year by the succeeding praetor. The standard Edict became very large, and we know of about two hundred separate provisions (or edicts) of the Edict as it was stabilized in the Empire under Hadrian. The

8. *Digest of Justinian* 9.2.1.1.
9. *Asinaria* 371.

very great majority of these edicts certainly originated in the Republic, though in the course of time many underwent modification. The Edict contained, in addition to these edicts, the form of action which governed a remedy allowed by the praetor, whether under an edict or under the civil law.

The importance of the Edict is enormous. As we shall see in later chapters, it influenced all areas of private law and in some, such as succession, was mainly responsible for the developed law. An illuminating instance can be drawn here from family law. Only the head of a Roman family could own property; hence, for instance, sons in their father's power and slaves could own nothing of their own. If a son or a slave made a contract, all the rights went to the father or master, and he could sue the other contracting party. But if this third party had a grievance he had no right of action against the father or master. It was felt to be wrong that the head of a family should suffer loss through the fault of his dependants. This rule, which was intended for the benefit of the head of a family, began to have the opposite effect because no one in his right senses would make a contract with a son or slave since he could be sued by the father but would have no right of action against the father. Slaves could not be sued at all; sons could, but they had no property. A series of edicts improved the situation. They declared that if the father had told the third party that he could make the contract with the son or slave, the father was completely liable on the contract up to the amount which he had specified; or if the father had made a profit on the contract he was liable up to the limit of his profit; or again, if the father had given the son or slave a fund to administer as if it were his own *(peculium)* the father was liable up to the limit of the fund. Provision was also made by other edicts for cases where the son or slave (or other person) was set up in business or put in charge of a ship by the father, and for deciding what was to be paid out of the son's or slave's fund to the father and what to other creditors. In practice these provisions meant that sons and slaves could be used to make commercial transactions, but the father was saved from having to make good their worst excesses.

The praetor's influence on the development of the law was not restricted to the Edict. In individual cases he could grant an action when none existed at civil law or under the Edict. There are few instances of this practice in the Republic, but it was quite common in the Empire. Likewise from at least 70 B.C.[10] the praetor could in a particular case

10. Valerius Maximus, 7.7.5.

refuse to allow an action to be brought although it was permitted by the civil law.

Beside the urban praetor was the peregrine praetor, whose office was created in 242 B.C. His activities in the legal sphere are regarded as being concerned with cases involving parties at least one of whom was not a Roman citizen. He too issued an Edict, and we know that to a large extent this corresponded to the Edict of the urban praetor. He is, indeed, usually given the credit for the most important legal advances. Law which concerned foreigners as well as Romans, it is said, must be simpler, hence the pressure to simplify law would be greater on the peregrine praetor than on the urban praetor. Foreigners, it is alleged, could not take part in the old kind of formal legal procedure *(legis actiones),* hence the simpler type *(formulae)* introduced at some time by a praetor was meant for them; and the rigidity of the other system was such that the development of law for Roman citizens themselves lagged behind. It was not until the Aebutian law *(lex Aebutia)* of about 140-120 B.C., it is held, that the new procedure became widely available for cases involving Romans alone, yet this is after the introduction of the famous consensual contracts[11] (to be mentioned in a moment), so, since they are praetorian, they must be the invention of the peregrine praetor. But these arguments for the paramount importance of the peregrine praetor are not nearly so strong as they appear at first sight. The foreigners, who at this early period would be near enough to Rome to take advantage of or suffer from Roman courts, would normally be fairly prominent merchants, and it is doubtful whether the commercial law would need to be much simplified for their benefit. Again, foreigners could have appeared in court under the old formal procedure by means of the ingenious fiction inserted into pleadings telling the judge to proceed as if they were Roman citizens: this fiction is well known, it seems very old, and it is difficult to see any other use for it. Also there are strong indications of consensual contracts in Cato's work on agriculture[12] which was written around 160 B.C. for Romans, and so these contracts–and hence wide use of the more recent informal procedure–must then have been available to Roman citizens.

The truth is that we know virtually nothing about the respective spheres of operation of the urban and peregrine praetors, though we do know that as magistrates they were of equal rank. Cicero[13] tells us that the edict against robbery with violence was issued by Marcus Lucullus in 76 B.C. and that its object was to put down the violence which was

11. Which cannot have existed under the old formal procedure.
12. *De agri cultura* 144-150.
13. *Pro Tullio* passim.

rampant in Italy after the Civil War. This is expressly stated. But by 76
B.C. those who lived in Italy were virtually all Romans, yet Lucullus was
peregrine praetor, not urban praetor. Again, the edict against fraud
which Cicero describes (with some exaggeration) as "the dragnet for all
wickedness"[14] was the creation of Aquillius Gallus, presumably in 66
B.C. when he was a praetor. He was certainly never urban praetor, yet
there is not the slightest indication that originally the edict did not
operate when citizens alone were involved.

Whoever deserves the credit, urban praetor or peregrine praetor, a
Roman praetor seems to have been responsible for the first introduction
of consensual contracts. These are contracts which are valid simply
because of the agreement of the parties, not because of any writing or
any other formality or external requirement. This idea of making agreement itself the binding element of a contract, simple though it looks, is
a great achievement: even at the present day no legal system has consensual contracts except those which have borrowed them directly or in-
directly from Rome. The Romans recognized four consensual contracts
–sale, hire, partnership, and mandate–and in all probability the first three
at least were in existence before the beginning of the second century B.C.

The other important Edict is that of the curule aediles, who were the
magistrates in charge of the streets and marketplaces at Rome. The
provisions of their Edict are mainly important in the development of the
law of sale,[15] though other clauses concerned such things as the keeping
of wild animals near streets in such a way that they might cause injury.
It has been suggested that the main provision on sale dates from 199 B.C.,
but whether this is so or not, this Edict was known to, and parodied by,
Plautus during the early second century B.C.[16]

Statutes and Edicts need to be interpreted, and much of their effect
and influence will depend upon the way they are interpreted. In Anglo-
American law the important work of interpretation is done by the judges
deciding upon actual individual cases. In Roman law it was done by the
jurists, who would consider both actual and imaginary cases.

At first, interpretation of law in general was completely in the hands
of the College of Pontiffs. But although this was a religious body with
religious functions it has already been observed that to be a pontiff was
to hold public office and was a normal part of a prominent Roman's
career. So far as we know, the pontiffs were not particularly chosen for
their religious outlook, but until the Ogulnian Law *(lex Ogulnia)* of 300

14. *De natura deorum* 3.30.74.
15. Cf. below, pp. 69-70.
16. *Captivi* 802ff.

B.C. only patricians could be pontiffs,[17] and until 253 B.C. no plebeian was elected chief priest (pontifex maximus). The pontiffs gave advice as to what the law was to the magistrates and to the people. This gave them—and through them the patricians—enormous influence, especially because of the paucity of statute and (at this time) of the Edict, and because they controlled the forms of action (that is, the technical requirements for bringing lawsuits). They used their powers of interpretation as circumstances demanded—they could make a provision wide or very narrow. To achieve their object they were prepared to misinterpret the original provision *deliberately*. Their most famous piece of interpretation is of a clause of the Twelve Tables[18] which repeated a law of Romulus:[19] "If a father sells his son three times let the son be free of his father." Originally this was meant as a restriction on the powers of insensitive fathers. The head of the family (paterfamilias) had complete power over his sons and could sell them. If he sold his son into civil bondage and the son was released, the son fell back into the power of his father—hence the statute to restrict the rights of unfeeling fathers. But in course of time it came to be appreciated that a man who was free of his father's power had great advantages: he would himself be a paterfamilias and could own property, and so on. Fathers at times wanted their sons—as a mark of esteem—to be free from their power, and this provision of the Twelve Tables was used to achieve their aim. The father would sell his son to a friend who would immediately transfer him back; this procedure would be gone through again; and then after a third sale by the father the son would be released by the friend, and he became a paterfamilias in his own right. So far so good. But the pontiffs went much further. The Twelve Tables' provision had said nothing about the sale of daughters or grandchildren, presumably either because they were included under the term son or because it was intended that no matter how often they were sold, they would always on release fall back into the power of the paterfamilias. But the pontiffs decided that the Twelve Tables' provision meant that for sons three sales by the father were necessary for release from paternal power, that this restriction was not expressed in respect of daughters and grandchildren, and hence they were freed from the father's power, once and for all, by *one* sale. In ways such as this, statutes could be reinterpreted to meet new and unforeseen circumstances.

According to tradition, this monopoly of the pontiffs over the interpretation of laws was broken at the end of the fourth century B.C. when

17. Livy 10.6.3ff.
18. 4.2.
19. Dionysius 2.26, 27.

Gnaeus Flavius, secretary to Appius Claudius Caecus, the censor of 312 B.C., stole from his master (with his master's connivance) a catalog of the all-important forms of action and published them.[20] In reality, the loss of power by the pontiffs is likely to have been much more gradual and less dramatic, since the forms of action were no closely guarded secret. If they had been, Appius Claudius would not have known them since he was never a pontiff.

The next major step in the history of the jurists was the publication of a book called *Tripartita* by Sextus Aelius Paetus (consul in 198 B.C.), who, with his brother, is the first known nonpontifical jurist. The *Tripartita* was apparently the first law book to do more than simply give a collection of the forms of action, and it seems to have been so called because each topic was divided into three parts: the clause of the Twelve Tables, then the interpretation of it, and third the relevant form of action.

The jurist Pomponius (writing in the second century A.D.) tells us that Quintus Mucius Scaevola, the consul of 95 B.C., was the first jurist to arrange the civil law into *genera,* classes.[21] This probably means that he attempted some kind of rationalization, that he tried to draw distinctions between related topics and was interested in classification. His writings were numerous–nearly 180 books, according to Pomponius–and his most important was a commentary in 18 books on the civil law. This was the first systematic legal treatise, and it became the basis of most later works on the civil law. He thus heralds the era of modern law at Rome, and his work was carried on by his many pupils.

With the advent of this new era and the turn of the century comes a political change. Previously the jurists were virtually all men of the senatorial class. Now the knights take over and the nobility more or less disappear from the ranks of the jurists. These jurists of the first century B.C., according to Cicero,[22] had three main functions: *ad respondendum,* to give advice when consulted both by individuals and by judges who at that time were not trained lawyers; *ad agendum,* to help conduct lawsuits; *ad cavendum,* to draft documents. This last function was very important at this early period and established many principles of form and interpretation which continued centuries later. For instance, the form devised by Cicero's contemporary, Aquillius Gallus, for the complicated task of appointing as heir the testator's unborn grandchildren by a son who died before the testator, was still standard in the time of

20. *Digest of Justinian* 1.2.2.7.
21. *Digest of Justinian* 1.2.2.41.
22. *De Oratore* 1.48.212.

Justinian, six centuries later. In contrast to the Empire,[23] drafting was regarded as a serious matter fit even for the consideration of the leading jurists. We know of one situation when four of the most important jurists, Labeo, Ofilius, Cascellius, and Trebatius, were consulted.[24]

The jurists of this period continued to exhibit the freedom of interpretation which has already been noticed. To take two examples: The Twelve Tables gave a remedy when a man's land was injured by work done on neighboring land which diverted rain water *(aqua pluvia)* onto his property. Trebatius held that the action would lie when the damage was caused by hot springs.[25] Again in a situation when a remedy was available when something was done by force *(vi)*, Quintus Mucius Scaevola held that it was done by force when a person did it who had been told not to.[26]

The last century of the Republic was the most fruitful period of Roman legal development; hence the emphasis on the later Republic which will appear in subsequent chapters.

SOURCES OF WRITTEN LAW IN THE EMPIRE

The Emperor Augustus claimed to have restored the Republic, but though the sources of law at first sight appear unchanged, they underwent fundamental alterations.

The *comitia* continued to be able to legislate. Indeed, under Augustus it passed several laws concerning the family which were of great importance; but these were all part of Augustus's policy for reforming Roman morals, and all the statutes were passed at his request. In succeeding reigns a few statutes were passed, especially under Claudius, who was emperor from 41 to 54 A.D. But here as elsewhere, Claudius showed himself an amateur of earlier days and out of step with the mood of his time. By the end of the century, legislation through the *comitia* had died out.

Likewise at first no change was made in the power of the magistrates to issue new edicts, but they stopped doing so. We do have evidence that occasionally praetors made slight modifications in the Edict, but no substantial change in the law was brought about by the praetor through his Edict in the Empire. This is in astounding contrast to the feverish activity of the last two centuries of the Republic. During the reign of the Emperor Hadrian (117-138 A.D.), the jurist Julian was given the task of

23. *Digest of Justinian* 28.2.2.29 pr.
24. *Digest of Justinian* 28.6.39 pr.
25. *Digest of Justinian* 39.3.3.1.
26. *Digest of Justinian* 50.17.73.2.

revising the Edict of the urban praetor. How much he changed is not known–probably very little–but we know that he made one important modification in the form of the Edict and one minor alteration in the substance. But henceforward no urban praetor could make any change in the Edict. Presumably, though we have no direct evidence, the peregrine praetor and the curule aediles lost their power to make new edicts at the same time.

The jurists continued to play an important role, but they were skillfully controlled by the emperor. Augustus gave certain selected jurists the right to make replies to legal questions on his authority *(ius respondendi).* The exact import of this is not precisely known, but in all probability it means that when one of these jurists gave an opinion it would not technically be binding upon the judge but in practice it would always be followed. This grant of authority not only enhances the value of an opinion by such an honored jurist; it devalues the opinion of all the others. The value of a juristic opinion therefore depended upon the emperor's favor. Hadrian took matters a step further and said that the opinions of such jurists had the force of law if they all agreed, but the judge could follow whichever opinion he pleased if they disagreed.[27] Exactly what this meant has been a source of great controversy among modern scholars, and an improbable variety of opinions has been expressed. None is obviously right, and in view of the conflict any might be followed.

The first 250 years of the Empire was the great period of juristic activity. Book after book was produced in profusion by one famous jurist after another. These books might be complete commentaries on the whole of the Edict or on the whole of the civil law, or they might be monographs on one branch of law. Or they might be collections of replies to problems, whether actual problems or theoretical ones invented by colleagues or pupils, or they might, like Gaius's *Institutes,* be students' textbooks. Justinian later claimed that his *Digest* resulted from the consultation and condensation of two thousand such books. These juristic writings developed law in a variety of ways. Important problems could be under discussion for centuries. For instance, the contract of sale provided excellent remedies, so many jurists wished to extend the scope of the contract. We know that the question of whether barter, exchange of goods for goods, was sale was vigorously fought for generations. New problems were raised and answers given. The rationalization of these affected in turn the answers given to old, well-known problems. Statutes

27. Gaius *Institutes* 1.7.

were interpreted and reinterpreted. For the first century and a half the
jurists were divided into two schools, the Sabinian and the Proculian,
which probably were actual teaching establishments.[28] But all in all, the
jurists of the Empire were less daring in their interpretations and modifications of the law than their colleagues in the Republic had been. Perhaps the increased volume of law rendered such daring less necessary,
perhaps as a result of experience they were more aware of the dangers
of too great freedom of interpretation, but also perhaps, like the magistrates who of their own accord stopped issuing new edicts, they were
afraid to be bold.

New sources of law also developed in the Empire. Decrees of the
senate *(senatusconsulta)* had no lawmaking force during the Republic,
but from the beginning of the Empire it became common to enforce
senatusconsulta by means of a clause inserted into the praetor's Edict.
Eventually, even without the intervention of the Edict, *senatusconsulta*
began to have direct lawmaking force. The first certain instance is the
senatusconsultum Tertullianum of Hadrian's time, though it is from
time to time suggested that there are earlier examples.

Though the early emperors did not have legislative powers, their
right to legislate was completely accepted by the middle of the second
century A.D., and it seems to have developed from no legal foundation.
Gaius says it was never doubted that what the emperor decides has the
force of law because he receives his authority *(imperium)* by law.[29] And
the later Ulpian says that the emperor's decisions have the force of law
because, by the law passed concerning his *imperium,* the people gave him
all their *imperium* and power.[30] Gaius's explanation takes us nowhere,
and in the statute to which Ulpian seems to refer there is no indication
that the people delegated their authority to the emperor.

Imperial constitutions fall into four main groups. The emperor could,
like any other high magistrate, issue edicts, but since his powers were not
limited to any particular sphere he could issue edicts on any subject and
concerning any territory. For instance, the *constitutio Antoniniana* of
212 A.D., which gave Roman citizenship to all free inhabitants of the
Empire, was an imperial edict. Again, individual lawsuits would come
on appeal before the emperor, who acted as supreme judge. Naturally,
his decisions *(decreta)* were treated as extending beyond the individual
case. Then too, legal problems might be addressed to the emperor by

28. Though no doctrinal difference between the schools can be found, their continuing
and continued disputes were invaluable for development.
29. Gaius *Institutes* 1.5.
30. *Digest of Justinian* 1.4.1 pr 1.

officials or public bodies or even by private individuals, and the imperial chancellery would issue replies *(epistulae)*. The emperor's instructions *(mandata)* to his officials and especially to the provincial governors also came to have binding effect for the future.

It is convenient here to say a few words about Roman actions. Actions were of fundamental importance in Roman law since one had a legal remedy only in situations when an action was provided. In general Roman actions were individually tailored to fit each distinct institution. In early times legal proceedings were by what were called actions of the law *(legis actiones)*. There were only a limited number of these and they were very inflexible. Gaius believed that if the slightest mistake were made in the form of words used, the case was lost. Though it seems that Gaius is not accurate, the fact that he could make this mistake is itself significant. The actions of the law were very restrictive, and they came to be replaced by what is termed the formulary system *(formulae)*. The stages of this development are much disputed, but it seems that in many cases some actions could be by *formulae* as early as the beginning of the second century B.C. Most of the *legis actiones,* however, also continued in existence for some considerable time. The *formulae* were very much more flexible and could be adapted to many new needs. In particular their relative informality meant that they could play a role in the shaping of new informal institutions such as the consensual contracts, and that in some actions, prominence could be given to the good faith of the parties.

IV

FAMILY LAW

BETROTHAL

IN EARLY TIMES reciprocal promises of marriage were exchanged on behalf of the bride and bridegroom. The promises took the form of the contract of *sponsio*[1] and they were actionable. By the beginning of the second century B.C., though these promises were still made–or at least, one was given promising the girl–the right of action had disappeared. Since the form of betrothal was unchanged and the *sponsio* in general was still actionable, the only explanation is that the Romans had decided that it was immoral to allow an action for breach of promise of marriage. It seems that a dodge was tried to circumvent this conclusion. Instead of the girl's being promised in marriage to the young man, the promise would be to pay a fixed sum if the girl failed to marry the young man. But this, too, was declared unenforceable.

The promise on behalf of the young man would be by his father, or by the young man himself even if the father was alive. The promise of the girl was always by the head of her family, the paterfamilias. If the girl was not under the control of a paterfamilias the promise would always be given by one of her relatives. These relatives would have no power over her, and it is reasonable to imagine that their intervention was due to social, not legal, reasons. It was considered improper for a woman to promise herself in marriage. Although breach of the promise was not actionable, betrothal had certain legal consequences: sexual intercourse with another man by the girl constituted adultery; the relatives of the pair had the status of in-laws from the first moment of betrothal.

Through the agency of Christianity, Jewish law had profoundly modified Roman forms of betrothal by the fourth century A.D. The fiancé now gave the girl a gift *(arra sponsalicia)* to insure the betrothal. If he did not marry her he forfeited the gift; if she refused to marry him she

1. See below, chapter 7, under Verbal Contracts.

31

had to return at first fourfold, in later times double, the amount of the gift.

MARRIAGE

Roman marriage was of two types. The older, marriage *cum manu,* put the wife under the power of her husband (or his paterfamilias if he had one); she was in the legal position of a daughter, and any property she owned now belonged to him. In the later type, marriage *sine manu,* the wife remained free of her husband's power *(manus)* and continued to be in the power of her own paterfamilias, or to be independent if she had none.

The three ways in which a marriage *cum manu* was created were all fully established by the time of the Twelve Tables. The first was by *confarreatio,* a religious ceremony which required the presence of a leading priest. The name derives from the cake of spelt *(far)* which played a prominent part in the ceremony. Even if this form was not restricted to the aristocracy by law, it was in fact. The second way, *coemptio,* purchase, was a particular application to marriage of *mancipatio,* a formal mode of transferring certain kinds of valuable property. *Mancipatio,* as we shall see, was one of the most vital institutions of Roman law. Starting as a mode of transferring property, it came to be used to create servitudes over a neighbor's land and pledges of property, to make wills and marriages, to adopt children, to free children from the paternal power, and to obtain a new and less strict guardian for a woman. *Coemptio* is in the form of an imaginary sale of the woman to her husband, and it is likely that in very early times it was an actual sale.[2] The third way was by *usus,* use. If a wife remained with her husband for a year at a time and did not absent herself from him for three successive nights she fell into his *manus.* In this case the marriage was valid before the *manus* was created.

The other type of marriage, that *sine manu,* was fully established as civil law marriage from an early date and was quite common by the beginning of the second century B.C. The scarcity of sources does not allow us to decide how much older it is as a type of marriage rather than as the first period of a marriage on its way to becoming a marriage *cum manu* by *usus.* No ceremony or formality was necessary for this, though it appears that in the Empire the wife had to be led to her husband's

2. For the form of *mancipatio* see below, chapter 6, under Acquisition of Ownership.

house. What distinguished marriage from concubinage was the intention of the parties, and this was usually indicated by a provision for dowry.

It would seem that Roman wives more and more began to feel constricted under the power of their husbands. Still, even if they did not take part in the ceremonies of *confarreatio* and *coemptio* they would fall into their husbands' power automatically if they did not take the precaution of absenting themselves each year for three nights. It can be shown that at the beginning of the first century B.C. marriage *cum manu* was still very common. Yet, almost overnight, in Cicero's time the situation changed. The reason can be seen in Cicero's speech in defense of Flaccus, where he argues that a certain married woman had not been in the power of her husband and especially not as a result of *usus* since, he says, "nothing can be taken away from a woman's property rights without the consent of all her guardians."[3] The point is this: when a woman was not subject to the power of her father or husband, any property she had was controlled by guardians and she could not transfer any important piece of property *(res mancipi)* without her guardians' consent. This was a rule of the Twelve Tables, and originally it applied only to deliberate acts of alienation by the woman. The situation of a woman (and hence her property) entering into the power of her husband automatically as a result of living in marriage with him for one year was not covered, and was never meant to be covered, by this provision. But once it was widely felt that women ought not to be so subject to their husbands in the old sense, this provision was deliberately misinterpreted. The result was that a woman no longer automatically became subject to her husband's power by living with him for one year, but only if her guardians consented. After it had been accepted that women who were not in their fathers' power did not fall automatically into their husband's *manus* by *usus,* the rule would soon be extended to women in the power of their fathers. In the early Empire legislation abolished *usus* completely. The other forms of marriage *cum manu* also became rare. Certain high priests had to be born of parents married by *confarreatio* and had to be so married themselves. It became so difficult to find persons qualified for the priesthood that Augustus and his successor Tiberius issued legislation that *confarreatio* would not affect the wife's civil position but would only transfer her to her husband's family for religious purposes.

A valid civil law marriage could be contracted only between Roman citizens or with persons of a state with which Rome recognized the right of intermarriage. A slave could not marry. Marriage between patricians

---

3. *Pro Flacco* 34.84.

and plebeians was recognized by the *lex Canuleia* of 445 B.C. In the Republic there was no legal ban on marriage between freeborn citizens and freedmen, but such a marriage was looked upon unfavorably and punishment might be exacted by the censors. (The office of censor was first created in 443 B.C., and the censors had the job of preparing the lists of citizens made every five years, largely for military and tax purposes. Since the censors decided to which class in the state a citizen belonged, they could move one of whom they disapproved from a higher to a lower class, or put a black mark against his name. The censors used this position of power to become the guardians of Roman morals, and they would intervene, for instance, if a father abused his power over his children.) Augustus introduced legal restrictions on marriage when he enacted that senators and their descendants could not marry freedmen. In the later Empire Jews and Christians were forbidden to intermarry.

The consent of the paterfamilias of both the bride and the bridegroom was required, and it seems that in early law, though not in the Empire, the wishes of the girl were–legally–entirely irrelevant. When the paterfamilias was dead, no outside consent was required either for the man or for the woman, though the tutor of the woman would have to consent to the constitution of a dowry. When the marriage was *cum manu* by *confarreatio* or *coemptio,* the woman's tutor's consent was needed. As we have seen, in Cicero's time the tutor's consent also became necessary for a marriage *cum manu* created by *usus.*

Close relationship was a bar to marriage, though the prohibited degrees varied from time to time. In ancient law, marriage between second cousins was forbidden, but in Cicero's day first cousins could marry. Uncle and niece and great-uncle and great-niece could not intermarry. The Emperor Claudius (41–54 A.D.), who wanted to marry his niece, Agrippina, laid down that marriage with a brother's daughter was lawful, though he did not validate marriage with a sister's daughter. Three and a half centuries later the old rule was restored. Another instance of the law being changed to suit the matrimonial convenience of the leaders of state concerns the marriage of the Emperor Justinian. Augustus's *lex Papia* had forbidden those of senatorial rank to marry actresses without the emperor's permission. The Emperor Justin, so that his nephew Justinian could marry Theodora, allowed marriage with retired actresses. In 542 A.D., Justinian himself abolished all these restrictions on senators' marriages.

From at least the time of Augustus the minimum age of marriage for a girl was fixed at twelve, and whether or not puberty had been reached was irrelevant. There is evidence that marriage before puberty was not uncommon for girls. As for males there was a dispute between the rival schools of jurists. The Sabinians demanded that the boy should have reached puberty, and a physical examination was required. The Proculians, whose view prevailed, demanded only that the boy be fourteen.

Marriage, unless it was *cum manu,* had scarcely any effect on the status of the husband or the wife. The husband in early law had the right to punish his wife severely–but we cannot tell whether before Augustus's legislation this right was restricted to marriage *cum manu* or applied to all. The main effect of a valid Roman marriage was that the children were legitimate and were under the power *(patriapotestas)* of the head of the family.

DIVORCE

The right of divorce was recognized at Rome from the earliest times. It was common in the later Republic and, despite Augustus's moral legislation, in the early Empire. At the time of the kings it seems that a husband could divorce his wife for adultery, for tampering with the keys, or for poisoning a child.[4] If he divorced her, she and her father had no right to reclaim any dowry which had been given with her. If the husband expelled her from the matrimonial home (or, it may be, divorced her) for any other reason, he had to give her one half of all his property. These provisions seem to have survived for a long time, and they were still in force about 230 B.C. when the famous case of Spurius Carvilius Ruga occurred. As it is reported by the antiquarian, Aulus Gellius: "In the book which he wrote *On Dowries* Servius Sulpicius also says that private agreements for the return of dowry seemed necessary for the first time when Spurius Carvilius Ruga, a man of noble birth, divorced his wife because as a result of a physical defect no children were born from her. . . . And the tradition is that this Carvilius dearly loved the wife whom he divorced and held her in great affection because of her character, but higher than his affection and his love he set the oath which was compelled by the censors that he would marry a wife for the purpose of begetting children."[5] This then was the situation. A virtuous but sterile wife was divorced when she had committed none of the precise offenses which would justify this act in law. But the husband was not acting badly either! He loved his wife, but set above all else the traditional oath which was given to the censors, the guardians of Roman morals, that he was marrying in order to beget children. Technically, he should now have to

4. See above, p. 11.
5. *Noctes Atticae* 4.3.1, 2.

give half of his property to his divorced wife–a hard decision, and the probability is that the penalty was not exacted. But then no legal action would be available against him for the recovery of his wife's dowry. The significance of the case did not escape the notice of the Romans. Henceforward it would be wise for prospective fathers-in-law and bridegrooms to make their own personal financial arrangements in case the marriage failed. Now a husband without penalty could divorce his wife for reasons other than those laid down by statute. The steps in the next development are very obscure, but the changes occurred very rapidly, long before the end of the Republic. A husband could divorce his wife without any grounds whatever, and equally a wife could divorce her husband unless she was in his power. The very heavy financial penalties for being the guilty party or for divorcing one's spouse without justification disappeared. Except when the parties had made their own arrangements, the wife's dowry had to be returned to her or her father if the marriage ended in divorce, but the husband was entitled to retain certain fractions of it, for instance if there were children of the marriage, and he could retain other fractions if the wife had committed adultery or was unjustifiably divorcing him. If the husband were at fault and not the wife, he would lose his right to keep any of the dowry.

No ceremony or formalities were necessary for divorce unless the marriage had been constituted by *confarreatio.* Then a reverse ceremony, called *diffarreatio,* was needed.

The law of divorce in the later Empire also has particular interest. It is a curious fact that although the Roman Empire became Christian in 325 A.D., there is hardly any evidence that Christianity affected the substance of Roman private law, whether for good or evil. Divorce is the most notable exception to this. Constantine, the emperor responsible for the conversion of the Empire, enacted that if one spouse divorced the other (except for certain specified causes), then in addition to the existing penalties affecting the dowry, an offending wife could be deported and an offending husband could not marry again. If he did remarry, the divorced wife could seize the second wife's dowry. The law underwent various changes in the next two centuries. The Emperor Justinian in the sixth century provided that if a wife divorced her husband and not for one of the recognized reasons, she was to be confined to a nunnery for life and have all her property forfeited. A husband who divorced his wife without good reason was subject only to financial penalties. Even here Christianity had so little effect on the fundamental structure of the law that in all these cases, despite the penalties, the divorce itself was valid.

DOWRY

Something has already been said about the return of dowry at the end of a marriage. Dowry was created in three ways: by delivering it *(dotis datio)*, by promising it under the contract of *stipulatio (dotis promissio)*, and by *dotis dictio*. This last was the most restricted way since it could be used only by the paterfamilias of the bride, the bride herself, or a debtor of the bride. In it the father of the bride (or whoever it was) would open proceedings by promising to pay a certain sum as dowry, and the bridegroom would signify acceptance. Its appearance is peculiar–and demands to be explained–since it is the sole Roman verbal form of agreement[6] which is unilateral (that is, creates obligations on one side only) and where the initiative is taken by the donor. The explanation of the form is to be found in its social setting. Originally, *dotis dictio* was made only at the time of betrothal. The prospective bridegroom would ask for the girl's hand. The father would promise her and with her a certain sum as dowry. The bridegroom would accept. It was obviously regarded as proper that the matter of the amount of dowry be first raised by the girl's father and not by the future husband. Legal effect was in time given to the social usage.

The wife's or the father's action for the recovery of dowry *(actio rei uxoriae)*, which came into existence after the divorce of Carvilius Ruga, is unique. The main part of the proceedings ran: "If it appears that Numerius Negidius (the husband) ought at civil law to return the dowry or part of it to Aula Ageria (the wife), Judge, condemn Numerius Negidius to pay Aula Ageria whatever of that sum is fairest and best: if it does not so appear, absolve him." In other words, the judge had to work in two stages. First he had to decide whether at law the husband had to return the dowry or part of it. Then, if so, he had to condemn the husband in whatever share seemed right.[7] Apparently, the judge could reduce the amount returnable to the wife but not increase it. This might happen when the husband had incurred reasonable expenses in connection with the dotal property. Another peculiarity of the action was that a father who had given the dowry could not by himself sue for its recovery, but the wife had to be joined as co-plaintiff.

PATRIAPOTESTAS

This was the most fundamental and most peculiarly Roman part of family law. Children born to parents validly married at civil law came

6. Apart from the very special *iusiurandum liberti.*
7. Thus, the amount of the condemnation could not exceed the value of the dowry.

under the power *(patriapotestas)* of the father, or under that of the father's father if he were still alive. This *patriapotestas* continued so long as the father remained alive. Even if the son reached the highest offices of state, he still remained under the power of his pater. The father had complete power of life and death over his children–though if he used his power arbitrarily he might be punished by the censors. He could sell them into slavery, his consent to their marriage was needed, and he could bring about their divorce if he wished. The children could own no property–though customarily they were given a fund *(peculium)* which they administered as if it belonged to them; anything they acquired belonged to the father. If the son made a contract, the father immediately acquired all the rights under it against the other party. But conversely, since it was felt to be wrong that a man should suffer harm through the acts of his children, he did not in early law become liable on the contract to the other party. The extent to which this last point was modified has already been described.[8] Important changes in the concept of *patriapotestas* occurred sparingly. The right to sell into slavery had disappeared before the beginning of the Empire. Augustus allowed a soldier son to keep as his own property anything he earned as a soldier *(peculium castrense).* The son retained ownership of it even after he left the service, except that he could bequeath it by will only so long as he was a soldier. This restriction was removed by Hadrian. Later under Constantine this same concept was extended to earnings derived from certain public offices *(peculium quasi castrense).* The same emperor also provided that what a child inherited from his mother should belong to the child though the father had the right to use it and its income so long as he lived. Antoninus Pius took away from the father the right to end a harmonious marriage against the wishes of his child.

   Patriapotestas was acquired not only by birth but also by adoption. Adoption took one of two forms. The first, *adoptio,* was that used when the person to be adopted was already under *patriapotestas.* Like *coemptio,* this was an adaptation of *mancipatio,* the form of conveyance for certain kinds of important property. The father "sold" the son three times and the "purchaser" freed him after each of the first two "sales." After the third *mancipatio,* the "purchaser" either remancipated him to the father or he retained him. The adopter would then go before the praetor and claim that the boy was his son, and the father or "purchaser" would put up no defense. The praetor adjudged the boy to the adopter

8. See above, p. 22.

as his son. The three sales by the father were necessary because of the rule of the Twelve Tables that a son was released from his father's power if the father sold him three times. There is no indication that a son, even fully grown, had to consent to his adoption. The other form, *adrogatio,* was used when the person to be adopted was not under *patriapotestas.* This form is more complicated, for religious reasons. Any male not under *patriapotestas* is himself a paterfamilias and, if he is adopted, his family will at once die out and there will be no one to continue the family's religious rites. The procedure took place in two stages. First, there was a preliminary enquiry by the pontiffs. They had to decide that the adopter was no longer able to procreate children–in classical law he had to be at least sixty unless there were special circumstances–and when he was able to, he must have tried.[9] If the pontiffs approved of the *adrogatio,* the matter went before the *comitia curiata* which for this purpose was named the *comitia calata.* Both the adopter and the person to be adopted were asked if they agreed to the adoption, and the people were asked to sanction the adoption. The form of the question put to the people shows that the ceremony was actual legislation, and we know that it was still so regarded in the time of Cicero.[10] The adopted person not only entered the family of the adopter; he acquired the status in the community which he should have as a son of the adopter. Thus, Cicero's enemy, the demagogue Clodius, was a patrician but wished to hold the office of tribune of the plebs which was open only to plebeians. Consequently he had himself adrogated by a plebeian. This principle was carried much further in early law than in the Empire. At one time–as late as the second century B.C.–a slave who was adopted became legally freeborn.

From the time of Constantine right up to the reign of Justinian there was considerable legislation allowing, in certain well-defined circumstances, an illegitimate child to be legitimized, and so to be put within *patriapotestas,* if the parents subsequently married.

Patriapotestas could be ended not only by death but also by the emancipation of the child. *Emancipatio* was useful for the child because it made him a paterfamilias. In *emancipatio* a further use of *mancipatio* was made. The son would be "sold" by the father the regular three times, and three times he would be reconveyed to the father. The father would then manumit him just as he would free a slave. Here too, only one sale was needed for daughters and remoter descendants.

9. Cf. Cicero *De domo sua* 13-14. 34-38.
10. *De domo sua* 16.41.

TUTELAGE

Both males and females who were not in *patriapotestas* and were
under puberty had the protection of at least one tutor. Tutorship was,
as many texts stress, a very sacred duty. According to Sabinus, it took
precedence over all other duties, over those to a guest, to a dependent,
to a relative.[11]

There were various kinds of tutors. First there could be a tutor
appointed by will *(tutor testamentarius)*. This type was well established
as early as the Twelve Tables. The only person who could appoint a
testamentary tutor was the paterfamilias, and he could appoint only to
his *sui heredes,* that is, to those in his power who on his death would not
fall into the power of another. The form of appointment was rigidly
controlled, and the testator had to use set forms of words, "I give Lucius
Titius as tutor to my children" *(L. Titium liberis meis tutorem do)* or
"Let Lucius Titius be tutor to my children" *(liberis meis L. Titius tutor
esto),* otherwise the appointment was void.[12] This type of tutelage continued even in the time of Justinian. Again, the Twelve Tables laid down
that when there was no testamentary tutor, the tutorship was to go to
the agnates, relatives linked through males, and this type also continued
into Justinian's time *(tutor legitimus).* All the nearest agnates in the same
degree of relationship who were themselves above the age of puberty
became tutors at the same time. These nearest agnates are also the
persons who would succeed to the property if the ward *(pupillus)* should
die. It is no coincidence that they are given the duty of looking after the
ward's property. About 210 B.C. the *lex Atilia* allowed the praetor at
Rome and a majority of the tribunes of the plebs to appoint a tutor for
a person who had none *(tutor dativus).* Similar appointments could later
be made in the provinces under the *lex Iulia et Titia.* A fourth type of
tutor was the *tutor praetorius,* who was appointed temporarily when
there was an action of the old formal type *(legis actio)* between the ward
and his ordinary tutor. In the time of Gaius it was not clear whether this
kind of tutor still existed.

Tutorship was a public duty and anyone appointed had to act unless
he was disqualified or could claim some exemption. The law on exemp-
tions is very detailed and was the subject of a number of monographs.
That by the late classical jurist, Modestinus, was in six books. Excuses
might be temporary or permanent and could range from ignorance to
holding high public office, from being already tutor to three children to

11. Aulus Gellius *Noctes Atticae* 5.13.5.
12. Gaius *Institutes* 1.149.

the claim that the tutor was named in the will because of the testator's enmity towards him.

The tutor had general control of the ward's affairs, and he was to act in the interest of the ward. There is no sign that the tutor had any powers over the person of the ward or had a decisive voice in, for instance, choosing his dwelling place. At different times various acts of administration such as the sale of land could not be performed by the tutor, but we need not consider the details. While the child was an infant (*infans,* literally unable to speak and so understood until the beginning of the fifth century A.D. when the term was used of a child under seven), he could perform no legal act, and everything had to be done by the tutor. When the ward ceased to be an infant, all his legal acts which might result in loss to him had to have the authority of the tutor. When the transaction imposed rights and duties both on the ward without the authority of his tutor and on the other party, an attempt to achieve fair results was made. If the ward wished to enforce the transaction he had to be prepared to fulfill his side of the bargain. If the ward had already performed, he had the choice of recovering what he had given or of suing on the contract. When a debt was paid to the ward without the tutor's authority, the ward's receipt was not valid, but if he then sued for payment of the debt, he had to deduct from his claim the money he still had or had spent in a sensible way.

Tutorship could be ended by the ward's attaining puberty or by the death of the tutor or pupil. If a testamentary tutor were successfully sued for fraud under the *crimen suspecti tutoris,* he ceased to be a tutor.

The ward was protected by a number of remedies. As early as the Twelve Tables, the *actio de rationibus distrahendis* lay against the *tutor legitimus* for twice the value of any property which he had embezzled. The action was limited in value in that it could only be brought after the tutorship had come to an end. The *crimen suspecti tutoris* lay against the testamentary tutor for fraud. It was established by the Twelve Tables, and this time the action could be brought while the tutorship was still in existence. More important than either of these is the action on tutorship, *actio tutelae,* of later law. This belongs to the small group of good faith actions–those in which the judge is told to find for the plaintiff in a sum equal to what the defendant ought to give or do in accordance with good faith–and there are indications that it is the oldest of these. So a date in the middle of the third century B.C. seems plausible. At first it lay only when the tutor was guilty of fraud, but sometime before the end of the classical period it was available even when the tutor had simply been negligent. From the beginning of the Empire, tutors other than those appointed by will or by the higher magistrates had to give security, on undertaking the office, that the property of the ward would be safe.

It was not only persons under puberty who had tutors. Women above the age of puberty who were not under *patriapotestas* also had to have a tutor. This type of tutelage is also very old, and the tutors were appointed in the same way as for children. Nonetheless the woman herself had powers of administration; and all that the tutor had to do was to interpose his authority when it was necessary, generally when the transaction could diminish the woman's patrimony. In classical law tutelage of adult women was unnatural, and there were various dodges to enable them to change their tutors. The principal one was another adaptation of *mancipatio.* A husband in a marriage *cum manu* could also provide by will that his wife should have the right to choose a tutor for herself. Further, an adult woman could, without her tutor's authority, do a number of things which an ordinary ward could not do. She could, for instance, give a good receipt, and she could transfer *res nec mancipi,* things which did not fall within what had been in primitive times the category of the most important things.[13] Moreover, in situations when the tutor's authority was necessary, a woman could compel the tutor to give it, unless he was a *tutor legitimus.*

CURATORSHIP

By a provision of the Twelve Tables which continued to apply in later law, lunatics were placed under the curatorship of their nearest agnates. An even older legal rule, which, however, is repeated by the Twelve Tables, declared that a prodigal who wasted an inheritance which had come to him on intestacy might be forbidden by a magistrate to deal with his property and placed under curatorship. Later, presumably also in the Republic, the rule was extended to cover the situation when the prodigal had inherited his property by will.

It will have been noticed that many of the rules of tutorship and of curatorship, especially in early law, seem to be for the protection of the property in the interests of the nearest relatives who would succeed to the estate if the person under tutorship or curatorship should die. Presumably this fact explains the lack of interest in early law in male minors over the age of puberty. A male, once he had reached the age of puberty, could make a will and so exclude his agnates from rights of succession. Moreover, he could marry and have children and on intestacy *they* would be his heirs.

13. See below, chapter 6, under Acquisition of Ownership.

The first special protection for minors was under the *lex Plaetoria* of 193-192 B.C., which provided a fine for anyone who should defraud a person under twenty-five. The same statute also provided a particular defense which a minor could put up if he was sued by a person who was defrauding him. The praetor also issued an edict for the minor's protection; the remedy here was available for any transaction when the minor might suffer loss. But it was only much later, around the second century A.D., that it normally became possible for a minor to have a curator who would be appointed if the minor requested it. As the system developed, a young man who had a curator could not be made liable on any of his transactions for more than he had gained, unless the curator had given his consent to the transaction.

V

SLAVERY

SLAVERY WAS a fact of Roman life and law from the early days of the city until well after the period with which we are concerned. ⸤How satisfactory the developed rules were for a slave state can be demonstrated by a glance at articles 172 to 196 of the Louisiana Civil Code of 1824, or at chapter 3 of Title 6 of the earlier Digest of 1808. Most of these provisions give in effect pure Roman law.

The main ways in which a person might become a slave were by capture from a people which did not have a treaty of friendship or a relationship of agreement with Rome, or by birth to a slave mother. It was established in classical law that if a slave woman was free at any time between conception and birth the child was free. There were other exceptional cases, too, when a child born to a slave woman would be free, such as when the owner was under an obligation to free the mother and had delayed in doing so. The Roman mentality shows itself in some of the other causes of enslavement. Under the Twelve Tables a thief caught in the act was enslaved. The state could sell into slavery those who avoided being enrolled on the census. Evasion of the census was used to avoid military service. During the later Republic the census began to be taken only rarely, but evasion of military service still carried this penalty. Persons sentenced for certain crimes were also enslaved. A free person who had himself fraudulently sold as a slave in order to share in the purchase price (on the assumption that later a friend would come along and prove that he was free) was, it was decided, actually to become a slave. Most instructive of all is the *senatusconsultum Claudianum* of 52 A.D. This declared that if a free woman cohabited with another's slave and the owner forbade it, the free woman and any child became the slaves of the male slave's owner. For this a magistrate's decree was necessary. The free woman could make a bargain with the slave's owner that she herself would remain free but any child born to her would be a slave. If the woman was in her father's power and he had not consented to the cohabitation, these rules did not apply. It was thought wrong that a father, without any fault on his part, should be deprived of a daughter. Where the woman in question was a freedwoman and her former master had not consented to the cohabitation, she became the slave of her former owner. The reason for this was that the former master, the patron, had residual rights of which he should not involuntarily be deprived. When the male was a slave of the state, then the woman–again subject to any right of father or patron–did not become a slave but an imperial freed-woman. Justinian abolished the rule of the *senatusconsultum Claudianum,* but he gave full authority to the master to punish the slave or bondsman.

A slave was in some ways regarded as a thing, in other ways as a man. Anything which a slave produced, for instance any earnings, went to the master just as did the produce of any other thing. But it was settled by the late Republic or early Empire that children born to slaves were not to be treated as fruit "for it seemed absurd to include human beings among fruits since nature procured the fruits of all things for the sake of human beings."[1] Despite the high moral tone of the argument–and the decision that human beings were not fruit must in fact rest on a moral or philosophical basis–the decision itself is not concerned with the slave's well-being. It does not mean that the children of slaves are free; rather, its practical application was that when some person not the owner became entitled to the use and the fruits *(usus fructus)* of a slave woman, any child born to her did not belong to the usufructuary but to the slave's owner.[2] Like other things, a slave could be stolen, but certain wrongs could be committed in respect to a slave though not in respect to other things. Thus an action would lie for insult to a slave *(actio iniuriarum)* or for corrupting his morals *(actio servi corrupti).* A slave could own no property, but from early times it was customary to give the slave a fund which he could administer as if it belonged to him *(peculium).* Technically, this sum belonged to the master, but to some extent it was treated as a separate estate with which the master did not interfere except for good reason. At first when a slave entered into a contract on behalf of his master, he bound the other contracting party to his master but the master himself did not become liable on the contract. The steps by which within certain limits the master's liability was recognized have already been related.[3] When a slave committed a civil wrong the master had the choice of either paying the compensation fixed by law or surrendering the slave to the victim. This was to restrict the master's liability for the

1. *Digest of Justinian* 22.1.28.1.
2. See above, p. 5.
3. See above, p. 22.

slave's behavior to the value of the slave. A similar rule existed for damage by sons and by animals. The slave himself could neither bring an action nor be sued.

During the whole of the Republic the slave was legally at the complete mercy of the master. Only in the Empire were restrictions imposed on the master's power. The *lex Petronia* of the early Empire prevented masters' punishing slaves by making them fight wild beasts, unless a magistrate's authority was obtained. Claudius (41-54 A.D.) decreed that if a master abandoned a slave who was sick, the slave became free and had what were called Latin rights though he did not become a Roman citizen. Hadrian (117-138 A.D.) enacted that without a magistrate's consent a master could not kill his slave. Antoninus Pius (138-161 A.D.) gave slaves the right to help themselves. He permitted cruelly treated slaves to take sanctuary in a temple or at a statue of the emperor. A magistrate was compelled to investigate, and if he found that the master had been cruel, the slaves were to be sold with the condition that they would not be returned to their old master. Under Constantine, if cruel punishment by a master resulted in the slave's death, it was treated as homicide. Still more legislation was passed later, and in Justinian's time the master could only administer reasonable punishment. It should be stressed that this humanitarian trend began long before the Empire became Christian, and there is no sign that the movement speeded up because of Christianity.

There were three ways of freeing (manumitting) a slave during the Republic; the whole topic was of particular interest to jurists. All three ways gave the slave not only freedom but also citizenship, a remarkable concession both in the ancient world and in more modern times. More interesting still, only one form of manumission existed as such, the others being adaptations of other institutions. The form of manumission created as such was manumission by will. The testator who wished to free a slave had to use certain forms of words. Very much later, perhaps not fully until Justinian's time, tacit manumission by will was recognized when the testator, without declaring the slave free, appointed him heir or tutor. Inevitably, during the Republic some masters wished to free their slaves in their own lifetime. There was no specific provision for this, but two ways of doing it were found. Every five years the censors prepared and issued a list of citizens. It became customary for a master who wished to manumit his slave to allow him to enroll himself on the list of citizens *(manumissio censu)*. Technically this does not seem to be an act of manumission, but the slave then appeared to be and was accepted as a Roman citizen. This method disappeared when the taking of the census fell out of use. The other method *(manumissio vindicta)* was an adaptation of the action–which goes back at least to the Twelve Tables–which anyone could bring when a free man was wrongly held as a slave. A master who wanted to free a slave would have a friend bring this action against him, claiming that the slave was really free. The master put up no defense, and the magistrate declared that the slave was free. Again, technically there is no manumission. The idea is that the slave has always been free and a Roman citizen. A Roman who manumitted a slave became his patron and had certain rights which will be mentioned shortly. In neither of these last two ways of giving freedom does it appear on the face of it that there has been manumission, and so the former owner should not be entitled to these rights. But it seems always to have been accepted without dispute and, indeed, without any discussion, that the former owner did have the rights of a patron. The illogicality did not worry the Roman jurists.

If a slave were informally manumitted, he remained a slave, but even before the end of the Republic the praetor was intervening to prevent the owner from exercising full rights of ownership. Various forms of informal manumission came to be recognized–giving the slave a letter which stated that he was free, or making a declaration before friends. Persons so manumitted remained slaves, and their only right was that if a master tried to force them to work for him the praetor would intervene. Their position was regularized by the *lex Junia Norbana* of the early Empire, which declared that they were free and gave them Latin rights but not citizenship.

The only form of manumission which could be subject to conditions was manumission by will. The testator might postpone the manumission for a period of time, or until the slave did a certain thing. As early as the Twelve Tables the position of such a slave *(statuliber)* was protected. That statute provided that a slave who was ordered by will to be free on the condition that he paid a certain sum to the heir, if he were sold by the heir, would gain his freedom by paying the sum to his purchaser. By classical law this rule had undergone modification: the slave was to be free any time the failure to fulfill the condition was not his fault.

Manumission, especially by will, was very common in the later Republic. Augustus feared that the large number of freedmen could not be easily assimilated. Accordingly he issued restrictive legislation. By the *lex Fufia Caninia* of 2 B.C. masters were allowed to manumit by will only a fixed proportion of their slaves. The proportion decreased as the number of slaves owned increased: thus, those who owned between two and ten slaves could free one half, between thirty and a hundred one quarter;

and never more than one hundred could be freed by will. The *lex Aelia
Sentia* of 4 A.D. enacted that the owner had to be above twenty or the
manumission was void, and the slave had to be over thirty or he did not
become a citizen, but, after the *lex Junia Norbana,* also of Augustus's
time, would be a Latin. In both cases if there was a strong and honorable
reason, an exception could be made if the manumission was approved by
a body called the *consilium.* The same law also provided that manumission in fraud of the owner's creditors was void, and certain classes of
disgraced slaves, if they were manumitted, did not become citizens or
Latins but were given a particularly low status *(dediticii).*

FREEDMEN

Freedmen suffered under certain disabilities of public law which we
need not consider and, after Augustus, they could not marry persons of
the senatorial order.

They also had certain duties towards their patrons. They had to show
respect *(obsequium).* This means, for instance, that a freedman could not
bring an action against the patron or a member of his close family which
could involve them in disgrace. Indeed, to bring any action at all against
such persons the freedman needed the consent of a magistrate. He could
not give evidence in a criminal trial against his patron, and when a slave
girl had been freed by the patron so that he could marry her she could
not refuse.

The obligations were not all on the side of the freedman, however.
The patron had to provide for the freedman in case of necessity; in
classical law he could not give evidence against the freedman in a criminal trial; and later he could not be compelled to give such evidence.
Above all, the patron was not allowed to treat the freedman as a slave.
The master was permitted to bargain with his slave that in return for the
gift of liberty the slave, once he was freed, would perform for him each
year a fixed number of days' work *(operae).* But the amount exacted
could not be excessive. Under both the Twelve Tables and the praetor's
Edict the patron was entitled to a share of the freedman's estate *(bona),*
if the freedman died without leaving children who had been in his power.

VI

PROPERTY

THE ROMAN JURISTS' DELIGHT in classification is well demonstrated in property law. Most of their distinctions can be proved to be at least as old as the first century B.C., and it is likely that the others are equally old. The first division in Gaius's *Institutes*[1] is into those things which are under divine law *(divini iuris)* and those which are under human law *(humani iuris)*.

Those under divine law are either *res sacrae* or *res religiosae*. *Res sacrae* are those things such as temples which are dedicated, under the authority of the Roman people, to the gods above. *Res religiosae* are dedicated to the gods of the underworld and are graves alone. A grave is made religious by the act of a private individual when he buries a body in his own land, provided the funeral is his concern. The Roman sense of property and proprieties was so strong that even burial made the ground holy only if proper concern for ownership was shown. Another class, sanctified things, *res sanctae*, was regarded as being to some extent under divine law. These were the gates and walls of cities, and climbing upon them entailed the death penalty. Things under divine law could not be owned. This means, for instance, that when a body was buried in a field, the actual burial place ceased to be owned though the rest of the field was unaffected. In harmony with this, actions for disturbance of a tomb *(actio sepulchri violati)* could be brought by anyone, not just by the relatives of the deceased.

Things under human law were either public *(res publicae)* or private *(res privatae)*. *Res publicae* were things belonging to the state, such as roads, navigable rivers, and harbors. River banks were owned privately but their use was public; anyone could tie up his boat to trees which grew there. Another classification described some things as common to all *(res communes)*: the air, running water, and the sea. According to one early classical jurist the seashore up to the high-water mark of winter tides was

1. Gaius *Institutes* 2.2.

49

public; according to a later one and to Justinian it was all common to all. No one could build on it as a matter of right, but permission might be granted by the magistrates to erect a shelter, which, however, would give no property rights in the soil.

Gaius next divides things into corporeal and incorporeal.[2] Corporeal things were those which could be touched. Incorporeal things were those which could not be touched and were rights, such as debts and most servitudes over land. The practical importance of this classification is that the most common method of transfer of ownership *(traditio)* required an actual physical handing over of the thing. This was impossible when the thing was incorporeal, and a different method *(in iure cessio)* had to be used.

Gaius's final classification into *res mancipi* and *res nec mancipi* –terms to be explained in a moment–leads to his discussion of acquisition of property.

ACQUISITION OF OWNERSHIP

It is primarily in this field that we meet the Roman distinction between civil law *(ius civile)* and the law of nations *(ius gentium)*. Some branches of law applied only to citizens, others were equally open to foreigners. This distinction was important in ownership and to a lesser extent in contract. *Res mancipi,* for instance, could be owned only by Roman citizens, and three forms of acquisition of ownership, whether of *res mancipi* or not, were open only to Romans. We will look at these forms first.

In historical times *mancipatio* was, in its ordinary form, the usual method of transferring *res mancipi. Res mancipi* were Italic land (which was usually land in Italy but might also mean land in a district which had received Italic rights); slaves; cattle, horses, mules, and asses (these animals were included from birth according to the Sabinians, only from the time they were broken in as draught animals or beasts of burden according to the Proculians); and the four oldest praedial servitudes.[3] In all probability this list is a fossilization of the situation of very early times when all valuable things had to be transferred by *mancipatio.* The list covers the most important things in a primitive farming community. For *mancipatio,* the transferor and the transferee appeared with the thing to be transferred (unless it were land which could be mancipated at a distance) before five witnesses who had to be male Roman citizens above

2. Gaius *Institutes* 2.12.
3. See below, this chapter, under Servitudes.

the age of puberty and before a sixth person who had the same qualifica-
tions and who held a bronze scale. The transferee grasped the thing, for
instance a slave, with his hand, struck the scales with a bronze (or
copper) ingot, and said: "I declare this man to be mine according to the
law of the citizens and let him have been bought by me with this bronze
and by these bronze scales." Though Gaius does not mention it, it seems
to have been customary to mention the purchase price in this declaration.
The transferor said nothing; his silence indicated his acquiescence. The
declaration itself is, of course, archaic. The bronze ingot and the scales
presumably date back to a time before the invention of coined money
when the metal actually was weighed out. This means that originally
ownership could be transferred only when the price was paid, and at the
time of the Twelve Tables it was laid down that ownership was transferred by *mancipatio* only when the price was paid or security for payment given. These restrictions were eventually felt to be inconvenient,
and they were circumvented by the jurists of the later Republic in a very
characteristic way. They added a further situation when *mancipatio*
transferred ownership immediately, namely when the seller relied upon
the faith of the buyer. But in every case when the seller participated in
the ceremony of *mancipatio* without receiving the price at once or taking
security for future payment, he was relying on the faith of the buyer.
Hence throughout the whole of the classical law the mere ceremony of
mancipatio transferred ownership. The distinction between *res mancipi*
and *res nec mancipi* died out in postclassical times and was formally
abolished by Justinian, who, however, ruled that in sale, delivery did not
transfer ownership unless the price were paid or security given.

   Mancipatio had an automatic guarantee that if the seller were not the
owner and the true owner evicted the buyer from the thing, the seller
would pay the buyer double the price mentioned in the *mancipatio (actio
auctoritatis)*. This guarantee could not be excluded directly by the agreement of the parties. Very early, though, a dodge developed to exclude
liability for this guarantee when desired by the seller and acceptable to
the buyer. The buyer would mention in the *mancipatio* not the actual
price but a ridiculously small price. Since the sum obtained from the
seller by the buyer if he were evicted was twice the sum mentioned, not
twice the true price, this took care of the problem. This could occur, for
instance, when a creditor to whom ownership of something had been
transferred as security sold the pledge when the debt remained unpaid.
It was common for there to be written evidence of the *mancipatio;* this
would state both the true price and the price declared in the *mancipatio*.
In early law again, the *actio auctoritatis* would lie only if the price had

been paid or security given. A similar automatic guarantee gave the *actio de modo agri* when the acreage of land sold was less than that stated in the *mancipatio.*

A second form of transfer of ownership, which could be used for *res mancipi* and for *res nec mancipi* (which were all other things), was called *in iure cessio.* This had the form of a collusive action of the old formal type *(legis actio).* The transferor and transferee would appear before the magistrate, the transferee would claim that the thing was his, the transferor who was the true owner would not put up a counterclaim, and so the magistrate would adjudge the thing to the transferee. Since the proceedings were technically a lawsuit, the magistrate's award should, like all other court decisions, affect only the parties to the action. But here as elsewhere, legal logic, once it had served its turn, was less important to the Romans than convenience, and the magistrate's decision was treated as meaning that the transferee was in actual fact the true owner. In exactly the same way *in iure cessio* remained long after the old formal actions disappeared. Since *in iure cessio* was rather cumbersome, it was used only sparingly, but it had to be used, as the sole possible method of transfer, when what was to be transferred was an incorporeal such as a servitude right.

The remaining type of acquisition of ownership which was restricted to Roman citizens was *usucapio,* usucaption, which occurred when a person had uninterrupted possession of land for two years–of other things for one year–provided certain conditions were fulfilled. These conditions underwent very considerable modifications in course of time, but the main ones in classical law were that the thing had to be capable of human ownership, that it must not have been stolen property, and that the possessor must have begun to possess in good faith, usually in the belief that he was owner. In postclassical times a new system was introduced when the passage of time–now fixed at ten years if the possessor and the actual owner were in the same province, twenty if they were not– did not make the possessor owner but extinguished the previous owner's rights. By Justinian's time this possession did give ownership.

The main way of acquiring ownership which was open to foreigners as well as to Romans was by *traditio,* delivery. Actual physical delivery– though no further formalities–was usually required, but less was demanded in the Republic than in the Empire. In the later Republic there was *traditio* if the buyer put his seal on the goods bought even if he did not actually remove them from the custody of the seller. But even in the Empire there were certain relaxations. Thus, there was what was called delivery by the short hand *(traditio brevi manu)* if the buyer had custody of the thing before the agreement to transfer ownership was made. Here the agreement itself was enough to transfer ownership. And ownership was transferred by delivery by the long hand *(traditio longa manu)* when goods stored in a warehouse were sold and the seller gave the buyer the warehouse key within sight of the warehouse. A more extreme form (perhaps unconnected with *traditio), constitutum possessorium,* may have transferred ownership first in postclassical times. This occurred when the parties agreed that despite the sale the seller was to retain physical control of the thing for the time being, perhaps under a contract of hire. *Traditio* was not enough to transfer ownership of a *res mancipi* but if, say, a slave were handed over without *mancipatio,* and the transferor brought the action claiming ownership, the praetor would grant the buyer a defense. Sometime before the end of the first century A.D., the praetor granted an action *(actio Publiciana)* which enabled such a transferee to recover the slave if he got into someone else's hands. And, of course, the transferee might usucapt after one year for slaves and other things, after two years for land.

The sources discuss a number of other possible ways of acquiring ownership. *Occupatio,* occupation, was the acquisition of a hitherto unowned thing, such as gems found on the seashore, wild animals, and goods taken from the enemy. In the Republic wild animals were acquired as soon as they were so wounded that they could be caught, but in the Empire actual physical capture was needed. Specification, *specificatio,* was the creation of a new thing–as when I make wine out of your grapes–and accession, *accessio,* was the joining of a minor object irrevocably to a major one–a painting to a board. All these methods of acquisition, but especially the last two, created difficult questions of title, but it is clear from the texts that the problems seldom came before the courts. The discussions illustrate the Roman delight in raising legal questions and in establishing principle and detail.

POSSESSION

A person had possession of something when he had physical control of it (whether personally or through someone acting for him) and intended to keep it. Possession, as we have seen, was important for usucaption but, more significant still, it was itself protected. There was a twofold reason for this. First, the person who has possession usually has a good title to the thing, so protection of possession is protection of the right to the thing. Second, when there is a dispute over a thing, protection of possession will render violence less likely since the person who has no possession will go to the courts for satisfaction rather than seize control of the thing by force. In an action the position of the defendant is better than the position of the plaintiff since it is the plaintiff who has to prove his case, and if he fails the defendant will retain the thing. Hence in a dispute over ownership or other rights in a thing it is useful first to settle who has possession, control, of the thing, for he will occupy the role of defendant. The quarrel will proceed further only if the other party raises an action against him. The Roman procedure for possession, by *interdicta,* usually protected the existing possession. But it might restore the possession to someone who had lost it, for instance if he had been thrown out by force. And in certain extreme cases possession might even be given to someone who had never had it.

When a person holds a thing in his own name he will usually possess. But when he holds it as a result of a continuing agreement, as for security for payment of a debt or under a contract of hire, it will depend on social criteria whether he is regarded as possessing or whether the other person to the agreement possesses through him. Thus, the pledge creditor did possess. But Roman law, which was capitalistic, favored the landlord, and so under a lease the tenant did not possess but the landlord possessed through him. It was regarded as impossible for two persons with different interests to possess the same thing. If you took possession of something I had been possessing, my possession was lost. But it could happen that one retained possession of something even without physical control. The standard instance of this is seasonal pasture–the occupant uses it for only part of the year, but during the rest of the year has no intention of giving up his rights.

Both the intention and the physical control were necessary for the acquisition of possession. This created difficult problems–the solutions to which are disputed–when a son or slave took control of a thing without the father's or master's knowledge. An analogous problem occurred when something was given to an infant who was regarded as unable to form any intention. As was frequently the case, a less stringent view was taken at the end of the Republic. Then some jurists at least would allow the infant to possess even without the knowledge and authority of the tutor, but this was denied later.

SERVITUDES

Land and buildings could be placed under a burden to neighboring property, which was called a praedial servitude. These burdens, with one exception, could not constitute a duty to do something but were limited to allowing the owner of the neighboring land to do something on the burdened land, or forbidding the owner of the burdened land from doing something. There were numerous types of servitudes, but the four earliest, *iter, actus, via,* and *aquaeductus,* were in a special category since they were *res mancipi. Iter* was the right to cross the neighbor's land, *actus* the right to drive cattle across, *via* the right to have a road across–the Twelve Tables laid down very precisely the dimensions of such a road if the parties had made no express agreement–and *aquaeductus* the right to have an aqueduct across the neighbor's land. That they were *res mancipi* suggests that in primitive times they were thought of as corporeal, as actually conferring some kind of ownership in the soil of the neighboring land. Later many other servitudes developed. One mentioned is the right to pass smoke from a cheese factory through the apartments above. A common one is the right to light–the neighbor is not to build higher on his property in such a way that the adjacent owner's light will be affected. The one which offended against the principle that a servitude could not impose a duty to do something was the right of support to a wall or roof. The owner of the burdened property had to keep his wall which gave the support in good repair. This servitude is another instance of the readiness of the Roman jurists to abandon principle when principle was inconvenient. This right of support would arise only when the wall already existed on the land to be burdened, and that wall would usually be beneficial to its owner. Hence the normal rule that the owner of the land in right of the servitude was responsible for the upkeep of the physical condition of the servitude was not fully appropriate, since this time the owners of both properties were benefiting from the wall. Thus, either the right of support could not be recognized as a servitude–which would be most inconvenient–or the servitude would have to be anomalous in one way or another. The jurists naturally chose the latter alternative, but for a long time there was a dispute as to what the rules of the servitude were to be.

The significant thing about a praedial servitude is that it was regarded as being attached to the land and not to the person. Hence, the servitude was not affected by the deaths of the persons who created it, and it continued whether one or both of these sold their land to someone else. In classical law, the four original servitudes could be created by *mancipatio,* and all of them could be created by *in iure cessio.* Since they were incorporeal rights *traditio* was not appropriate. By Justinian's time more informal methods of creation were admitted.

In addition to praedial servitudes there were also personal servitudes. These were rights over someone's property granted to another *person* usually for life, though a shorter period might be laid down. The most important was usufruct *(usus fructus),* the right to enjoy the use and take the fruits of something. This was usually created by will for the benefit of the widow: the testator would leave all his property to his children but would grant a usufruct of it to his widow for as long as she lived. The other personal servitudes were *usus,* the right to use but not to take the fruits, and *habitatio,* the right to live in a particular dwelling. *Usus* would often be of limited value. Thus, a grant of the *usus* of a flock of sheep would give the recipient the right to use them for manuring his fields, but no right to their wool, milk, or lambs.[4]

REAL SECURITY

In ancient Rome it was normal for a creditor to take security for a loan. Though personal guarantees by friends for repayment were more common, real security, the giving of a pledge or pawn, was well established from early days.

The first type to develop was almost certainly *fiducia.* This involved the transfer of ownership of a *res mancipi* by *mancipatio* or of anything by *in iure cessio* from the debtor to the creditor as security. It had many advantages for the creditor. Since he was owner, his protection was great, and if the debtor did not repay the debt the creditor could sell the pledge and give a full title of ownership to the buyer. The position of the debtor was not so happy since he was no longer owner and had to rely on retransfer when the debt was paid. Perhaps an even bigger disadvantage for the debtor was that he could not raise a second mortgage on the thing since it was no longer his. Still, there was one advantage for the debtor. Since the creditor was owner and hence so well protected, the creditor might be more willing to allow the debtor to retain physical control of the thing, especially because the law forbade the creditor to make use of things pledged. We can see from the texts, in fact, that it was usual for the debtor to be allowed to keep the thing under his control. When the debt was repaid the debtor had an action *(actio fiduciae)* against the creditor if he failed to restore ownership. There is usually felt to be a great mystery about this action since it should be very old and should have arisen during the time of the old and very formal strict procedure *(legis actiones),* yet it is very much an action relying on good faith.[5] And good faith actions, it is thought, can only have come into existence with the advent of the new informal procedure *(formulae).* The solution lies in the use made by the jurists of the Twelve Tables' provision on *mancipatio,*[6] "As the tongue speaks, so let the law be." The wording of the

4. *Digest of Justinian* 7.8.12.2.
5. Cicero *Topica* 10.42; *De natura deorum* 3.30.74.
6. 6.1.

mancipatio for security was altered slightly from the normal; the creditor declared that he was the owner and that the thing had been transferred to him and to his faith and trust *(fide et fiduciae)*. If the creditor did not return the thing an action would be brought by the debtor on the *mancipatio;* and, though the action would be one of strict law and would concern only the words used, these words themselves brought in the idea of the good faith of the creditor. Hence this good faith was relevant for the decision in an action of strict law. The jurists' attitude to this provision of the Twelve Tables was a big innovation since the clause was originally meant for the protection of the transferee, not of the transferor.

Next to develop was *pignus,* as when the debtor transferred possession but not ownership to the creditor. This too is quite old. Plautus, writing at the beginning of the second century B.C., makes a pun on *fiducia* and *pignus.*[7] If the creditor lost control of the thing he could not sue by the action claiming ownership, but a special action *(actio Serviana)* was early given to him for the pursuit of the thing whether it was in the hands of a third person or of the debtor himself. When the debt was paid, the debtor could always recover the thing from the creditor by bringing the normal action claiming ownership *(vindicatio)*. In addition, from quite early in the Empire he had a contractual action *(actio pigneraticia)* against the creditor.

Probably last to develop was *hypotheca,* though this was flourishing by the middle of the second century B.C. In this neither ownership nor possession was transferred to the creditor; however, he did have the same *actio Serviana* in respect of the thing if the debt was not repaid. *Hypotheca* was especially useful to the debtor because he could continue to use and benefit from the pledged object, and it was possible to give it in *hypotheca* to a second (or subsequent) person even before the first debt was repaid. It was, however, a criminal offense to make such a subsequent *hypotheca* without telling the new creditor of the previous *hypotheca.* If the debtor was unable to repay, the first creditor was entitled to have the full amount of his loan satisfied from the thing before the second creditor could claim anything due to him.

Strict rules, which varied from time to time, were laid down about the rights of a creditor to sell a pledge if the debt were not repaid.

---

7. *Epidicus* 697ff.

VII

CONTRACTS

MOST MODERN SYSTEMS of law have a general theory of contracts, that is, the parties may bind themselves by agreement for any lawful purpose in any way they like. Roman law is different. It has no general theory of contract but a number of individual contracts. An agreement, to qualify as a contract, either has to be made according to certain formalities–different formalities having different effects–or has to fall within a certain type which has a particular function. Each contract, therefore, has its own rules and regulations and consequences. Though there is a fundamental difference between Roman contract law and modern contract law, this is nonetheless the area in which Roman law has been most influential. Roman theory did in fact point the way to the modern development.

The *Institutes* of both Gaius and Justinian group contracts into four classes:[1] real, verbal, literal, and consensual. For us, though, it is more convenient to begin with verbal contracts.

VERBAL CONTRACTS

The oldest of these, and the oldest of all the Roman contracts, was *stipulatio* (or *sponsio*), which was in existence as early as the Twelve Tables of 451 B.C. This is quite remarkable proof of the Romans' genius for law, since contract–the state's recognition and enforcement of private agreements between individuals–normally develops relatively late. Stipulation was a formal contract, governed by strict law, and it bound only one of the parties. The formalities, though, were very simple. It was an oral promise in which the person to whom the promise was to be made asked the other if he would give or do whatever it was, and the other would promise using the same verb. The question and answer had to be exchanged orally, the promise had to correspond exactly to the question, and no delay was to intervene between the question and answer. This

1. Gaius *Institutes* 3.89; *Institutes of Justinian* 3.13.2.

means, of course, that the parties had to be face to face and the contract could not be made at a distance by letter. Originally there was only one verb formal enough to create the contract, *spondere,* to promise on one's oath. Only this form existed at the time of the Twelve Tables; and even later, right through classical law, this form had the peculiarity that it could be used by Roman citizens alone. The only exception suggested, says Gaius,[2] is that of the Roman emperor's using *spondere* when asking the ruler of a foreign state if he promises peace; or a foreign ruler's using it when he asks the same question of the Roman emperor. But, as Gaius says, this suggestion is over-clever. If this stipulation is broken, no court action arises: recourse to the law of war will alone suffice.

The history of *sponsio* before the Twelve Tables is obscure. Etymologically *spondere* is connected with the Greek word *sponde,* a libation made to the gods, and so it looks as if an oath was originally involved. One can conjecture that originally breach of the *sponsio* did not give rise to a legal action but to a religious sanction, and that at some later stage legal recognition was given. The first big development in historical times was an increase in the number of forms of verbs which could be used and the extension of the contract to foreigners as well as to Romans. This process apparently began early, and long before the period of classical law any verb at all could be used to make the promise.

It was said above that stipulation is a contract of strict law. What this means is that the parties to it are bound because of the form, and that the meaning of the agreement will be determined more or less completely by the words used. The promisor is bound even if he made a mistake or was forced into the contract by threats or entered it as a result of fraud. Naturally there were limitations on taking the wording too literally. In very early days it was recognized that if, as an actor on the stage, I made a promise to marry your daughter, I was not bound. The main consequence of the contract's being of strict law was that the parties were taken to mean exactly what they said and only what they said. Hence it was difficult to imply unexpressed terms into the contract. But even from early days some were implied. Thus, by the first century B.C. it was established that if I promised you I would do something and you made it impossible for me to do it, I was released from my obligation. Though the contract is so old, it was only in the first century B.C. that its most glaring faults–its validity despite threats or fraud–were tackled. This is typical of Roman jurisprudence. Institutions develop early, but once they do exist a strong legal conservatism acts against any radical change. Even

2. Gaius *Institutes* 3.94.

more significant in this respect is the nature of the remedies. These are totally separate from the stipulation, so that the contract remains unchanged in theory even though it was radically altered in practice. About 80 B.C. the praetor Octavius gave an action for four times the loss suffered when there had been extortion *(actio quod metus causa),* and he also allowed the injured party to be restored to the position he would have been in but for the transaction *(restitutio in integrum)* and gave a defense *(exceptio metus)* if the wrongdoer brought an action on the contract. Such an *exceptio* is a special defense inserted into the pleadings by the defendant when he is not challenging the accuracy of the plaintiff's claim but merely alleging that some other special circumstance must be taken into account. Here the person who took the stipulation brings an action on it, and the defendant does not deny the stipulation or its validity, but claims that the contract was extorted from him by fear. Thus this innovation means that the stipulation is still regarded as valid but its effects can be negatived. This defense must be specifically put in the pleadings *(formula).* In 66 B.C. Aquillius Gallus gave an action for fraud *(actio de dolo)* which awarded simple damages and also a defense of fraud *(exceptio doli).* These remedies were originally meant only to cover cases where a contract was involved, though they were soon extended to other situations.[3] Since the *actio de dolo* was allowed only if there was no other suitable action which could be brought, and fraud was already actionable in the good faith contracts, this new action must have been primarily meant to reform stipulation and the less important literal contract.

Not all stipulations, though, were valid. A stipulation was void if it was immoral, illegal, or impossible, or made subject to such a condition. An example of an immoral stipulation is a promise to give a free man when he became a slave. Stipulations to be performed after the death of one of the parties were regarded as void because it was felt to be "inelegant" that an obligation should begin with respect to an heir. Stipulations, such as "Do you promise to give after my death?" (or "after your death?"), "Do you promise to give on the day before I die?" (or "on the day before you die?"), "Do you promise to give to my heir?" were all void, the second one because the day before my death could only be determined after I had died. In time it was realized that such contracts could have their uses, such as for life insurance schemes, and though the law was so well established that it could not be directly changed by the jurists, they did decide that the form, "Do you promise to give me when I am dying?" (or "when you are dying?") was valid. This, they held, was

3. See below, chapter 8, under Fraud.

not a stipulation to be performed after death since the obligation came into existence at the last moment of life. Again, there could be no stipulation that a third party would do something or that the promisor would do something for a third party. The way round this was to cast the stipulation in the form of a penalty for nonperformance of a condition: "Do you promise to give me 100 if Titius does not give me 50?" or "Do you promise to give me 100 if you do not give Titius 50?" If the condition were not fulfilled the action on the stipulation could be brought against the promisor.

One of the great merits of stipulation was that it could be used for any type of transaction. Thus, it could be used to make a sale, or even to make a clause in a contract of sale, to create dowry, and so on. One of its most common uses was for a personal guarantee, suretyship. If the creditor wanted to be sure that he would get his money back, the debtor might have to find someone to pay in his stead if he failed. The Romans went in for personal security much more than we do; it was regarded as a moral duty to act as guarantor for a friend. The usual form was that after the stipulation was taken from the debtor, another was taken from the guarantor who promised to pay the same debt. In early law only two forms of words could be used for this purpose, *spondesne?*, "Do you promise on your oath?" and *fidepromittisne?* "Do you promise on your faith?" The form of words chosen made little difference, except that *spondesne* could be used only by Roman citizens. These promises, *sponsio* and *fidepromissio,* were valid only if the principal obligation was itself a verbal contract and only if the principal debtor was legally bound. The heirs of these guarantors were not liable on the contract. The *lex Furia* of about 200 B.C. enacted that *sponsores* and *fidepromissores* were to be free from their obligations after two years, and if there was more than one guarantor, each could only be sued for a proportionate share of the debt. The *lex Cicereia* of uncertain date laid down that any creditor who took such guarantees had to notify publicly in advance and declare both the cause and extent of liability and the number of *sponsores* and *fidepromissores.* If he failed, the guarantors had thirty days in which they could protest and have their obligation set aside. It would seem from these two statutes (and others) that much concern was shown for the protection of guarantors. Like some other pieces of social legislation these laws had an unlooked-for effect. Guarantors were now so well protected that it was scarcely worth a creditor's while to demand that personal guarantees be given. Hence people in need of money found it more difficult to find creditors willing to lend. Eventually the matter was set right when it was decided that another form of words, *fideiubesne?,* could create personal security which was unaffected by the statutes. There is no evidence for *fideiussio* in the Republic but it dates at least from the early Empire. It was soon the usual type of personal guarantee, and in Justinian's time it was the only type left. It was valid even when the principal obligation was not a verbal contract, and when the principal debtor was not legally bound. The heirs of the *fideiussor* were liable on the contract.

The action on a stipulation was called a *condictio*. The other types of verbal obligation are the promise of a dowry *(dotis dictio)*, which we have considered already,[4] and the oath of a freedman *(iusiurandum liberti)*, which was the undertaking given on oath by a new freedman that he would perform certain services for his patron.

In early law, performance did not discharge a contract. Legally it was irrelevant. What counted was a formal release of the obligation cast in the same form as the contract. The only one important in historical times is *acceptilatio,* the appropriate release for stipulation. The promisor asked "Have you received what I promised?"; the other replied "I have"; and the obligation was disposed of. This formality ceased to be necessary for the release of a stipulation, but it continued to be useful and was employed when the parties agreed that the promise should not be ex-acted, and the creditor wished to release the debtor from his obligation without any performance. Since the form of *acceptilatio* made it appear that the debtor had done what he promised, some tricky situations might arise. One case was that of a debtor who proposed marriage to a woman creditor and they agreed that the amount of the debt should be the wife's dowry. The man was released from the debt by *acceptilatio,* and he might then fail to marry her. In such situations it was usually held that one could look behind the form of the release to the real situation.

LITERAL CONTRACT

This is another strict law contract–also giving rise to a *condictio*[5] –but it was obsolete before the end of the classical period. It was still flourishing, however, when Pompeii was destroyed by the eruption of Vesuvius in 70 A.D.; much evidence for it has been recovered from the ruins. It depended for its existence upon the habit of a Roman pater-familias of keeping account books, and when this practice disappeared so did the literal contract. The practice of keeping account books died out about the third century A.D., most likely because a tax was placed

4. See above, chapter 4, under Dowry.
5. See below, this chapter, under Condictio.

upon transactions and the easiest way of avoiding the tax was not to keep accounts.

We cannot really say how old the literal contract is. It cannot be earlier than the habit of keeping account books nor later than the beginning of the first century B.C. when it is fundamental to a transaction described by Cicero. It arose by means of two entries in the creditor's accounts. First he recorded that an existing debt had been paid (when it had not), and secondly he recorded that a loan had (fictitiously) been made. Of these entries the second is the more fundamental, but both may have been necessary. It seems that the literal contract is not an original obligation but is an obligation into which an existing debt could be transformed. This might have many advantages for the creditor. For instance, it could provide better evidence of the debt, and whereas a good faith obligation gave rise to an action for an indefinite amount–whatever amount was "good and fair"–here the sum due was fixed. Gaius does not say so, but the debtor's consent must have been necessary for the transaction, and some of the documents recovered from Pompeii and Herculaneum seem intended to provide evidence of the debtor's consent. Presumably this consent would be granted in return for some concession, such as a longer time to pay than was allowed under the original contract.

The strict law nature of the contract is well illustrated by a story of Cicero.[6] About the beginning of the first century B.C. the Roman knight, Canius, wished to buy a small estate near Syracuse in Sicily. Pythius, a banker at Syracuse, said he had no estate for sale but invited Canius to use the estate which he had by the sea as his own, and asked him to a meal on the following day. Pythius then persuaded the local fishermen to fish in front of the estate on that day. Canius came to the meal and saw each fisherman in turn lay his catch at Pythius's feet. He asked for the explanation and was told that the estate was the center of the Syracusan fishing industry, and that the fishermen could not do without it. This excited Canius's greed, and he persuaded Pythius to sell him the estate at an exorbitant price. The appropriate entries were then made in Pythius's books. The following day Canius invited his friends to his new estate, and he himself came early. There was no sign of any fishing boat. Canius asked a neighbor if the fishermen had a holiday. "None so far as I know," was the reply, "but no one fishes here. And I wondered yesterday what was happening." Cicero finishes his account: "Canius was furious. But

6. *De officiis* 3.58ff.

what could he do? For my colleague and friend, Gaius Aquillius, had not yet produced his remedies for fraud."

The literal contract had two forms. In one the debtor remained the same but the cause of debt was altered, as from a contract of sale in the story of Canius. In the other, the debtor was changed and what you had owed me is now owed by Titius. Both you and Titius must have agreed to this. It appears that only Romans could be the creditors in a literal contract, but there was a dispute between the Sabinians and the Proculians as to how far peregrines could be debtors.

Justinian, in his *Institutes,* also has a section on literal contracts.[7] He declares that the old literal contract is obsolete, but if someone puts in writing that he has received money when he has not, and two years pass, then if he is sued for it he loses his right to put up the defense that the money was not given him. One is not to take account of any stipulation but only of the written acknowledgment, and so, says Justinian, there is still a literal obligation. This is in fact not really a contract. The existence of an I.O.U. constitutes proof, after a lapse of time, that the debtor did receive the money. Justinian's *Digest* says nothing of the literal contract. What has happened is that the stipulation has degenerated. The stipulation was an oral question and answer, and no other formalities were demanded. But in the nature of things, proof of the stipulation would be needed, and it was customary to have a written document setting out the terms of the stipulation. We have indications that as early as the Republic difficulties might be caused if written evidence of the stipulation was not available. Naturally the written document would grow in importance, and it would be tempting not to bother making the stipulation but simply to record that there had been one. This, in turn, if unchecked, could lead to the complete disappearance of the oral contract. Justinian's literal contract with its reference to the stipulation fits into this picture. Even more so does Justinian's rule that if a stipulation is recorded in a written document, then it is to be presumed that the oral stipulation was actually made, and the presumption can be rebutted only by showing that one of the parties was away for the whole day from the place from which the document is dated.[8]

REAL CONTRACTS

Contracts made when one party delivered something to the other were called real contracts. According to Justinian's *Institutes*[9] and mod-

7. *Institutes of Justinian* 3.21.
8. *Code of Justinian* 8.37.14.2.
9. *Institutes of Justinian* 3.14.

ern analysis there were four real contracts: *mutuum* (loan for consumption), *depositum* (deposit), *commodatum* (loan for use), and *pignus* (pledge). Gaius's *Institutes* give only *mutuum*,[10] yet as we know from the fourth book of his *Institutes*,[11] he was certainly aware of the existence of the other three. His failure to deal with them at all as contracts is considerable evidence that his *Institutes* are modeled on an earlier work, written before these contracts came into existence. *Mutuum* is very different from the others and much older.

Mutuum is a strict law contract of loan for consumption. It is unilateral; only the debtor is bound. He received the ownership of the thing lent, and his obligation was to give back something of equivalent quality. This meant that the contract was suitable only for things which are calculated by weight, number, or measure, such as money or grain, but not for things which have individual character such as horses or slaves. The action given was again the *condictio*, and interest could not be sued for on the contract. If the lender wanted interest a separate stipulation for it had to be made. The *senatusconsultum Macedonianum* of Vespasian's time (69-79 A.D.) provided that no action was available to anyone who lent money to a son in power, even if his father had since died. Macedo was apparently a young man who killed his father in order to get money to repay his debts, and the *senatusconsultum*, it was hoped, would prevent more such incidents.

Commodatum was loan for use and was very different from *mutuum*. Ownership of the thing did not pass to the borrower. Hence if the thing were destroyed, the loss did not fall upon him unless he had failed to show the degree of care which was thought to be appropriate. The contract had to be gratuitous; that is, the borrower gave nothing for the loan, or the contract would be one of hire. A praetorian edict gave a praetorian action for *commodatum (actio commodati)* before the end of the Republic, but in the early Empire there developed a good faith action at civil law which then existed side by side with the praetorian action. *Commodatum* shares this peculiarity of having two contemporaneous actions with deposit and *negotiorum gestio*, but no explanation of the phenomenon is satisfactory.

A good faith action is one where the judge was instructed to make an award against the defendant, if he found him liable, of a sum equal to what he should give or do in accordance with good faith. It allowed the judge to take a much more flexible attitude than was the case with

10. Gaius *Institutes* 3.90.
11. Gaius *Institutes* 4.47.

the strict law actions; above all, he could take into account matters such as fraud although there was no special clause to that effect in the pleadings.

Deposit *(depositum)* is the gratuitous handing over of a thing for safekeeping. Generally speaking, the person who took the deposit was only liable for fraud, not negligence, and he had to return the thing to the depositor on demand. The Twelve Tables gave an action for double damages for deposit; wrongful failure to return was apparently treated as theft. Later the praetor issued an edict which really has two parts: for ordinary deposit, fraudulent failure to return the thing gave rise to an action *(actio depositi)* for its value; for deposit resulting from riot, a house's falling down, fire, or shipwreck, the action was for double damages against the depositee or for simple damages against his heir. By the side of these provisions there developed the good faith action, probably in the Empire.

Pignus, pledge, has already been discussed.[12]

Consensual Contracts

Consensual contracts require no formalities but merely the agreement of the parties no matter how it is expressed. There were four: sale, hire, partnership, and mandate, and of necessity they were good faith contracts. They are of particular interest for they are so uniquely Roman. Accordingly, the question of their origins, especially of sale which appears to be the oldest, has been much discussed. One view is that sale derived from state practice. Booty captured from the enemy was from early times sold without formalities by one of the magistrates, and the sale was complete as soon as he accepted a bid made by a private individual. No legal action was available, but if a dispute arose the magistrate settled it on equitable grounds. This, it has been suggested, gave the Romans the idea that even between individuals prescribed formalities might not be needed. Another view is that sale was at one time a real contract and that a legal action would be available only if after the thing were delivered to the buyer he did not pay the price. But a difficulty here is that sale as a consensual contract seems to have been in existence from at least the beginning of the second century B.C., and the real contracts–apart from *mutuum* which is so different that it cannot have provided a model–are all of later origin. A third hypothesis is that the sale was made by the buyer giving the seller an earnest *(arra)* for the price. This was the binding element in Athenian law, and in Rome

12. See above, chapter 6 under Real Security.

it was also common for the buyer to signify agreement by giving some token or part of the price to the seller. But there is no evidence that *arra* had any legal function in Roman law before the time of Justinian. Another possibility is that the parties exacted from each other a stipulation or a series of stipulations which set out the terms of the contract. There was, the suggestion is, a gradual breakdown of the formalities, and eventually it was recognized that mere agreement was enough. Even in classical law stipulations played an important role in sale.

SALE. The essentials of sale *(emptio venditio)* were agreement, price, and a thing. No formalities were needed, but usually the contract would be put into writing or made before witnesses so that there would be some evidence. Justinian made a change in the law by enacting[13] that when it was agreed that the contract was to be made in writing, agreement did not make the contract complete, and for its validity the contract had to be put into formal writing. Until these formalities were completed, he decreed, either party could withdraw from the contract without penalty. But if an earnest *(arra)* had been given for the contract, then if the buyer withdrew he forfeited the *arra;* if the seller withdrew he had to restore the *arra* and as much again. Since agreement was so fundamental to sale, mistake which was sufficiently grave stopped the contract from coming into being. Mistake was regarded as sufficiently grave if it had to do with the thing sold, for instance if I think I am buying your slave Stichus and you think you are selling your slave Pamphilus; or if it was on some fundamental quality such as the material of which the thing was made, as when I thought I was buying a gold ring when it was made of brass. If I bought vinegar thinking it was wine, the sale was good if the vinegar was wine which had gone sour, but void if the vinegar had been specially made as such from other substances. The sale was also void if I bought a slave boy thinking he was a slave girl, but not if I bought a girl thinking mistakenly that she was a virgin. When the error was not serious enough for the sale to be void the buyer would have no remedy unless the error was due to the seller's misrepresentations. If these misrepresentations were innocent, the buyer's action *(actio empti)* would be for the difference between what he paid and the true value. If they were fraudulent, the buyer would also recover any incidental loss he might have incurred.

There had to be a price, and this, according to the Proculians whose view prevailed, had to be in coined money. The unsuccessful Sabinian view was that the price could consist of other things.[14] This dispute

13. *Code of Justinian* 4.21.17.
14. See Gaius *Institutes* 3.141.

between the schools lasted a long time. Sale was a very satisfactory contract and gave good remedies, and the Sabinians seem to have wanted to extend these remedies to barter, the exchange of things for things.[15] But the Proculian objection was unanswerable, namely that in sale the obligations of the buyer and of the seller were different, and that in barter one could not declare that one party was the buyer, the other the seller. The price also had to be certain, not in the sense that it must be known but that it is knowable and is not dependent upon some future event. For instance, a sale agreed to be for the price at which the seller bought is valid even though at the moment the buyer does not know how much that was and the seller has forgotten. But a sale at the price reigning in the market at Rome next market day would be void. The price, moreover, had to be a real price and the transaction could not be a disguised gift. This rule was needed since certain large gifts, especially between husband and wife, were void and a ridiculously low price might be set on a thing which was really intended as a present. A new rule came in with Diocletian (284-305 A.D.) but then disappeared until it was restored by Justinian, namely that if the price fixed was less than half the true value the sale could be set aside.[16]

Sale required a *thing* to be sold. Thus, if I sold you a slave who, unknown to either of us, was dead, the sale was void, and this was also the situation if I sold you a thing which in fact already belonged to you. A question of considerable interest to the jurists was whether there could be sale of things which could not be owned, such as of a free man or of religious, sacred, or public ground. The matter was of practical importance since such mistakes could easily occur, and originally the contractual actions would only be available if there was a valid contract. At first such sales were void. But there was a breakthrough in the early Empire when it was held that though the sale of a free man was void, nonetheless the contractual action *(actio empti)* would be available to the buyer. By the end of the classical period the jurists were saying that the sale of a free man was a valid sale though by it the free man did not become enslaved. The reason they give for this approach is the purely practical one that it is difficult to tell a free man from a slave. The next step was the recognition that the sale of a *res religiosa*–the place where a body was buried–was valid though the land remained *religiosa*. Again this was because it was difficult to tell this land from privately owned land. Before

15. See below, this chapter, under Barter.
16. *Code of Justinian* 4.44.2; 4.44.8.

the end of the classical period it was accepted also that *res sacrae* and *res publicae* could be sold.

The thing sold could be an incorporeal such as the right to an inheritance. But in this instance the person from whom the seller hoped to inherit must be dead, otherwise the sale was void for immorality. Future things such as next year's harvest could be sold. Such contracts could take two forms, either purchase of a hope *(emptio spei)* or purchase of a hoped-for thing *(emptio rei speratae)*. As to the first, what was bought was the chance, and for the sale's validity it did not matter that nothing materialized. An example in the texts is the next haul of a fisherman's net.[17] In the second instance, the future thing itself was sold and the sale was void if the thing did not materialize.

The obligations of the buyer and the seller were not the same. All the buyer had to do was pay the price on time, and if he delayed he had to pay interest on the price and the seller's expenses. The seller, on the other hand, had to keep the thing safe until it was delivered, he had to transfer quiet possession, he had to give warranties against eviction and hidden defects, and he could not have been guilty of fraud. A little more must be said about some of these duties of the seller.

The seller had to keep the thing safe until it was delivered. In Roman law, as we have seen, ownership was not transferred until the thing was actually handed over, but the risk of the thing's being destroyed or damaged was on the buyer from the moment that the contract was made perfect. Hence it was natural for the jurists to decide that if the seller who still had control of the thing did not look after it as he should, he would be liable to pay damages to the buyer.

But the seller did not have to give ownership to the buyer. The reason for this rule–which is contrary to modern law–has never been satisfactorily explained. At first, all the seller had to do was hand over the thing to the buyer; then if the true owner came along and recovered his property the buyer had no remedy unless the sale had been fraudulent.[18] So it became common for the buyer to protect himself by taking stipulations from the seller that the seller would pay him a certain amount if he were evicted from the property. These stipulations were so much a part of the standard practice that in Trajan's reign (98-117 A.D.) it was accepted that if the appropriate stipulation had not been given, the buyer could compel it by the sale action. Shortly afterwards the next step was taken, and the stipulation was simply assumed to have been given.

17. *Digest of Justinian* 18.1.8.1.
18. Unless the transfer had been by *mancipatio;* see above, p. 51.

So before the end of the classical period there was an inherent warranty that the legal possession of the buyer would not be disturbed.

Likewise at first the seller had no liability for hidden defects in the thing he sold. The buyer had to take it as it was. He could, of course, demand stipulations from the seller, but it seems that even before the end of the third century B.C. express statements by the buyer about the quality of the thing–even if they were not made as stipulations–would give rise to an action. The main development, though, was due to the Edict of the curule aediles who were, it may be remembered, the magistrates in control of the streets and marketplace at Rome. They issued an edict in the second century B.C. that the seller of a slave had to declare certain faults–mainly physical defects, but also whether the slave was insane, given to wandering away, or liable to noxal surrender.[19] If he did not declare any such faults or did not make good any express assurance made at the time of the sale, the buyer could bring an action within six months to have the sale set aside, or alternatively an action within one year to have the price reduced. Another clause of the Edict extended very similar provisions to the sale of beasts. There was, in effect, no way for the seller of slaves or beasts in the Roman market to avoid this liability, so it was really an automatic liability on the seller since it operated whether guarantees were given or not. A twofold development followed. First, the provisions of the Edict were widened, eventually including all things (even houses). Second, the scope of the Edict was widened so that it applied to all sales wherever they were made. This was the position that had been reached by Justinian's time, but it is not clear how much earlier it is.

HIRE. Little is known about the early development of hire *(locatio conductio)*. It was very wide in scope and covered hire of a thing, of work to be done, and of services. In early classical law it was disputed whether the payment had to be in coined money.[20] It was decided that it always had to be money, except that in the lease of a farm the rent could be fixed as a proportion of the produce.

When a thing was hired out *(locatio rei)*, the lessor did not have to be owner. He only had to give the lessee control of the thing for the agreed period. Hence subletting was possible, and in the case of apartments it was indeed common. If the thing was not fit for the purpose for which it was leased, the lessee did not have to pay the rent; but if the lessor unnecessarily produced the result that the lessee could not use the

19. See below, chapter 8, under Noxal Liability.
20. Gaius *Institutes* 3.144.

thing, the lessee was also entitled to recover any loss he might have suffered, for instance in a sublease. This question was often discussed: when the lessee was able to use the thing but something went wrong and he did not reap the expected benefit, what was his position in law? The texts instance situations when a crop is eaten by a plague of mice or of starlings, or the wine which has been made turns sour, or the land itself disappears during an earth tremor. The jurists decided that if the enjoyment was lost as the result of *vis major*, force which could not be resisted, then the lessee was excused from paying his rent, but not otherwise. In very late law, if the crop was very poor, the tenant did not have to pay his rent, but he would have to make it up in following years if the later crops were particularly good.

In hire of work to be done *(locatio operis faciendi)*, the person hired agreed to produce a certain result on a person or thing supplied to him by the hirer. For instance, I might agree to train your slave to be a doctor, or to make a ring out of your gold. Here the person hired was liable for any injury caused to the thing, or its loss, unless this was the result of *vis major* or robbery with violence, and it did not matter that the one hired was not negligent. He was also liable if he did not have the proper skill for the work undertaken.

Hire of services *(locatio operarum)* was not so important in the Roman world as it is today since a great deal of work was done by slaves, and for a free man to work for pay was rather looked down upon. Indeed, what were called liberal arts–the teaching of philosophy, practice of medicine, surveying, giving of legal advice, and so on–if practiced by free men, could not give rise to the contract of hire.

PARTNERSHIP. Partnership *(societas)* has a long history and can be traced, as a legal concept, far back beyond the introduction of the consensual contract. The earliest form was called *ercto non cito,* "when an inheritance has not been divided." This was not contractual but occurred automatically when someone died leaving a number of descendants who became his heirs *(sui heredes)*.[21] They were partners until the inheritance was divided, and it seems that frequently they decided not to split up the estate but to continue as partners. Since the partnership occurred in this way, it would be a partnership of all the property of the partners; even under the consensual contract such an unlimited partnership remained the standard form if not the most common. *Ercto non cito* must have been a very satisfactory institution, for at some later time the praetor allowed persons who were not *sui heredes* to enter into such a partner-

21. See below, chapter 9, under Testamentary Succession.

ship. This was the first contractual partnership, but it was not the consensual contract and it was set up by a judicial process. In turn this was replaced by the consensual contract. Roman consensual partnership was much wider in scope than partnership is today. Basically, it might take one of three forms: partnership of all the assets of the partners, a partnership for one kind of business, or a partnership for one transaction. The first could cause special problems of division of assets when it ended, for instance if one partner had married and had received a dowry which he might have to return when the marriage terminated. In that case, it was decided, the dowry went to the married partner and did not count towards his share of the assets.

Each partner could contribute assets, his work, or both, and there was no need for the contributions of the partners to be equal. But unless it was specifically agreed otherwise, every partner shared equally in any profit or loss. During the Republic there was a dispute as to whether it could be agreed that one partner was to take a greater share of profit than he would of any loss, and it was decided that it could.[22]

Partnership was ended by lapse of time if a fixed date for termination had been agreed upon, by renunciation by a partner at any time, by the death of a partner, or by any partner's bringing the contractual action *(actio pro socio)* against another. Each partner had to show good faith toward the others; the action was given only for fraud. It was felt to be a man's own fault if he chose a negligent partner.

MANDATE. *Mandatum* derives from the Roman idea that friends have a duty to help one another. It was the gratuitous undertaking to do something for another, and as a consensual contract it was certainly in existence before the end of the second century B.C. All kinds of activities could be the object of mandate and, unlike modern agency, it did not necessarily involve the agent in entering contractual relations with another. The mandate could not be for an immoral purpose, nor could it be wholly in the interest of the agent. The agent's duty was to perform his undertaking properly. Since it was gratuitous, the agent was normally liable only for fraud. The principal had to reimburse the agent for any expenses and also for any loss which he suffered.

That concludes the treatment of the main Roman contracts. Only these appear in the *Institutes* of Gaius and of Justinian. The main limitation of the system was that for an action or other remedy to exist there had to be a precise type of contractual relationship. In time this was remedied, at least to some extent. The *Digest* contains a title called *de*

22. Gaius *Institutes* 3.149.

praescriptis verbis, which seems rather confused but which deals with a number of contractual situations. The obligations of this title came to be known in the Middle Ages as the Innominate Contracts, an odd description since some of them do have names. The obligations here fall into two classes: those concerned with standard situations and which develop their own rules and have their own names, and those which do not concern such standard situations, when no named contract develops but an action is given. The most important of the former class is barter, *permutatio,* which seems to have developed into a contract in its own right in the first century A.D. This is exchange of goods for goods, and the contract was formed when one party performed his side of the bargain. More significant for later development, though, is the second class. A text of Paul, a jurist of the second century A.D., says that an action will lie on any agreement of the following four types, provided the person who wishes to bring the action has done his share: I give that you give, I give that you do, I do that you give, I do that you do. This is an enormous advance towards a general theory of contract. Now any agreement which imposes obligations on both sides will give rise to an action if one party has done his share. Another development to generalize contractual obligations was at work as early as the Republic. This was by means of pacts, *pacta,* agreements which did not fall into any of the classes of contract. At first these had no effect whatever. But sometime during the Republic the praetor issued an edict that he would protect pacts; by this he meant, not that he would allow an action on a pact, but that he would allow a pact to act as a defense. Thus, if I informally promised to pay you something and then did not pay, you could not sue me. But if you were bound by stipulation to pay me something and I informally agreed that you need not pay, and then I sued for payment, the informal agreement would be used as a defense to prevent my action's succeeding. In the Empire certain standard pacts even gave rise to a right of action.

It is convenient to deal in this chapter with two particular actions, the *condictio* and the *actio negotiorum gestorum,* though their connection with contract is tenuous.

CONDICTIO

In the action of *condictio,* the plaintiff simply claimed that something ought to be given by the defendant to him. The reason for the claim was not stated in the pleadings. Normally the action could only be brought if there had been a transfer of ownership from the plaintiff to the defendant (but there were exceptions, as in the case of stipulation); there must be no reason the defendant should retain the thing; and the object of the action had to be certain, either a particular thing or a fixed sum of money. In the contractual sphere this was the action available for stipulation, the literal contract and loan for use *(mutuum)*. It is reasonable to imagine that the right to an action was available here even before these institutions were regarded as contracts. They were all situations in which the defendant had something which he should hand over to the plaintiff. The *condictio* was also available when there was no contract; for instance, for the recovery of money which the plaintiff had given to the debtor and which he had mistakenly thought he owed him, or for the recovery of money given on the understanding that the recipient would give or do something in return and he failed, or for the recovery of money given for an immoral purpose when the immorality of the recipient was greater than that of the giver. For this last situation it should be observed that money given to a prostitute could not be recovered, on the sophisticated argument that it was immoral for her to be a prostitute but, being a prostitute, it was not immoral for her to take money. In one very anomalous case a *condictio* was even given to the person who was in fact the owner. This occurred when something had been stolen and its owner had the choice of suing for its recovery either by the normal action claiming ownership *(vindicatio)* or by the *condictio*. The most likely explanation of this oddity is that in very early times the *condictio* had a much wider range than it had later, and that, because of the hatred for thieves, the original scope remained in this one instance.

ACTIO NEGOTIORUM GESTORUM

The *actio negotiorum gestorum* cannot be regarded as a contractual action in any sense. But in early classical law it was available in a wide range of situations when one person looked after another's affairs, and it lay between the agent and the principal. This was the action given to or against the *cognitor*–the man appointed to take over the whole conduct of a lawsuit from one of the parties; the *procurator omnium bonorum* –the general agent appointed to look after all of a man's affairs; the *negotiorum gestor*–a person who, without being asked, intervenes to look after someone's property; the *institor*–a man set up in business on behalf of another; and the *curator*–the guardian of prodigals, lunatics, and later of minors. The action goes back to the Republic, and its history is obscure, but it is another case when there was a civil law action and an action under the praetor's Edict. Again there is no satisfactory explanation of the phenomenon. We do not even know for what kind of situation the action arose originally. Since the *Digest* title on it appears in Book

3, which is otherwise concerned with matters of court procedure, it is usually felt that the action must originally have been thought of in connection with representation in court. The argument is weak: this is the first appropriate place for the action to be discussed, and it might have been there for that reason alone.

VIII

DELICTS

IN ROMAN LAW many wrongs which nowadays would be regarded primarily as crimes gave the injured party a right to a civil action. The four main delicts, and the only ones discussed in the *Institutes* of Gaius and Justinian, are theft *(furtum)*, robbery with violence *(rapina)*, damage to property *(damnum iniuria datum)*, and personal injury *(iniuria)*.

THEFT

The delict of theft is at least as old as the Twelve Tables, which drew a distinction between manifest theft *(furtum manifestum)* and nonmanifest theft *(furtum nec manifestum)*. Manifest theft occurred when the thief was caught in the act; the penalty for a slave was to be beaten and thrown from the Tarpeian Rock, for a free man to be beaten and delivered as a slave or bondsman to the injured party. Later the praetor's Edict established that whether the thief was free or a slave, the penalty would be four times the value of the thing stolen. For nonmanifest theft the action was always for double the value of the thing stolen. The severe penalty for manifest theft is usually explained as either an inducement to the injured party not to kill the thief caught in the act but to have recourse to legal proceedings, or the result of certainty that the person apprehended is the thief. The Twelve Tables laid down that it was lawful to kill someone thieving at night, and only in the second century A.D. did this become unlawful if the killing was unnecessary.

Modern continental and Anglo-American law requires for theft that the thing be actually moved. This was also true of early Roman law, but, probably because Roman law did not regard attempted wrongs as actionable, the law widened and theft was committed by mere touching. This caused difficulties, especially since the damages were fixed as a multiple of the stolen thing's value. Thus Ulpian says, "It is a common question whether a person who moved a small quantity from a heap of grain commits theft of the whole, or only of what he takes away. Ofilius thinks he is a thief of the whole heap; for Trebatius says that even a person who

76

touches a slave's ear has touched the whole man. Likewise a person who opened a cask and took away a little of the wine is regarded as the thief not just of what he took, but of the whole cask. But in reality they will be liable on the action for theft only for what they removed."[1] Ulpian, who was writing in the later second century A.D., seems to be moderating the harsher opinion of these Republican jurists. Perhaps the most extreme instance given in the texts is that of a cargo of wine carried not in jars but free in the hold of a ship and someone's sucking some up.[2]

The taker had to have a wrongful intention and wish to make a gain. But, once more unlike modern Anglo-American law, he need not intend to deprive the owner permanently of the thing. Because the action was for a multiple of the thing's *value,* this rule, too, could operate harshly. Thus, someone who borrowed a horse for a journey and rode it further could be sued–unless he thought the owner would not have objected–for twice the horse's value.[3] The Romans themselves regarded these rules as harsh,[4] and in the situation when I drove your mule among my mares for breeding purposes only and with no intention of keeping it, Ulpian illogically held that there was no theft.[5] Certain persons who were not owners but were regarded as having an interest in a thing legitimately worthy of protection were also given an action for theft, but they were awarded only a multiple of their *interest.*

The Twelve Tables established a ritual search for stolen property *(lance et licio)* when, according to Gaius, the searcher was to be naked except for a loin cloth and had to carry a platter. If stolen property was found after this search, the theft was treated as manifest. The praetor's Edict introduced an action with a fourfold penalty when a search was prohibited *(actio furti prohibiti).* When, without the formal search, stolen property was found on a man's premises, the penalty laid down by the Twelve Tables was for three times the value, and the action lay whether the householder was the thief or not *(furtum conceptum).* The householder had an action for the same amount against the person who placed the thing there *(furtum oblatum).* These last two actions were later reiterated by the praetor's Edict.

ROBBERY WITH VIOLENCE

Rapina became the subject of a separate action when the peregrine

1. *Digest of Justinian* 47.2.21 pr.
2. *Digest of Justinian* 47.2.21.5.
3. Gaius *Institutes* 3.196.
4. Aulus Gellius *Noctes Atticae* 7.15.1.
5. *Digest of Justinian* 47.2.52.20.

praetor of 76 B.C., M. Lucullus, issued an edict to deal with it after the
Civil War. The action was for fourfold damages. What, however, was
unclear and the subject of much dispute was whether, as in the case of
theft, the injured party could also bring an action for the recovery of his
property in addition to this action.

DAMAGE TO PROPERTY

The subject of damage to property was mainly covered by the *lex
Aquilia,* a plebiscite of 287 B.C., though there are indications that this
statute consolidated earlier legislation. Only the hypothesis that the last
of the three chapters of the statute is an addition to earlier legislation
which consisted of the first and second chapters will explain the position
of chapter two sandwiched so illogically between one and three. Chapter
one dealt with the killing of slaves and beasts of the kind which go in
herds. Chapter two gave an action against an *adstipulator* who released
the debtor and defrauded the creditor. Chapter three gave an action for
other cases of injury to property, including the wounding of slaves and
cattle.

Let us look at chapter two first. An *adstipulator* was a friend of the
stipulator (creditor) and at the time of the stipulation he took another
stipulation for the same money from the debtor. The debtor was released
from his obligation when he satisfied either the principal creditor or the
adstipulator. In early times there was no contractual remedy between the
creditor and the *adstipulator,* and hence if the *adstipulator* released the
debtor but fraudulently did not hand over the money, the creditor was
left without a remedy. This was the gap filled by chapter two which,
however, became obsolete in classical law because the contract of mandate then governed the relationship between the creditor and the *adstipulator,* and the *actio mandati* was thought to be more satisfactory.

Chapter one of the *lex Aquilia* gave an action when a slave or four-
footed animal of the kind which go in herds was killed willfully or
negligently. The action was for the highest value which the slave or
animal had had during the past year; on occasion the owner might get
more than he lost, for instance if a slave was blinded, thus dropping in
value, and was later killed within the year. Herd animals included sheep,
goats, horses, mules, elephants, camels, pigs (after some hesitation), but
not dogs. In the first century A.D., though not before, the statute came
to be interpreted restrictively, and it was held that killing was different
from furnishing a cause of death. For the former, which alone gave rise
to the *actio legis Aquiliae,* the death had to be caused directly by the body
to the body. Apparently absurd distinctions were drawn. Thus, when a

pregnant woman died, it was killing if the midwife had administered a drug with her own hands, but if she had given it to the woman for her to take it herself this was merely furnishing a cause of death.[6] The Sabinians even went so far as to say that there was no killing if someone threw another's slave from a bridge into the river where he drowned.[7] But in all the cases when a mere cause of death was furnished the praetor would automatically grant an action on the facts though none was envisaged under his Edict or at civil law.[8] Indeed, it is in connection with the *lex Aquilia* that these praetorian actions on the facts are most common. The reason for this restrictive interpretation is not known. Nothing in the wording of the statute seems to account for it, and killing was not so narrowly viewed under other statutes. Presumably there was some practical reason for preferring to allow an action on the facts though we have no idea what it was.

Chapter three gave an action in the case of other damage caused negligently or willfully by burning, snapping, or breaking *(urere, frangere, rumpere)*, for the amount of loss which became apparent within thirty days of the injury. This restriction to the loss apparent within thirty days early ceased to have any meaning. At first the chapter seems to have covered only injuries to slaves and cattle, but it was soon made to apply to all things; the word *rumpere* was understood as meaning *corrumpere*, to corrupt, and to include all ways of causing damage. But in this chapter, too, the same kind of restriction to direct injury appeared in the Empire. Thus, if a ship was damaged because you cut its mooring rope, the *actio legis Aquiliae* would not be given, though there would be an action on the facts.[9] Under all three chapters a defendant who denied liability and lost his case had to pay double damages.

PERSONAL INJURY

Iniuria was the subject of three provisions of the Twelve Tables. If a limb was completely destroyed, the injured person could exact vengeance if the parties did not reach some financial compromise. For a broken bone an action could be brought for 300 *asses* if the injured person was a free man, 150 if he was a slave. For all other injuries an action lay for 25 *asses*. The fall in the value of money caused the last two provisions to lose most of their worth. Aulus Gellius recounts that a certain Roman used to stroll around, followed by his slave who carried

6. *Digest of Justinian* 9.2.9 pr.
7. Gaius *Institutes* 3.219.
8. See above, p. 22.
9. *Digest of Justinian* 9.2.29.5.

a bag of money; the Roman would punch whomever he fancied, and the slave would hand over the 25 *asses*.[10] Eventually the praetor issued a general edict on the subject, sometime before the end of the third century B.C.[11] Damages were now to be assessed by the judges. At first this action lay only for physical assault, but before the end of the second century B.C. the jurists had extended it to cases in which no blow had been struck. P. Mucius Scaevola, the praetor of 136 B.C., gave this action to a poet insulted from the stage.[12] Later when there was no physical assault, this action was used as an instrument of social policy. For instance, a creditor could recover from either the debtor or one of the guarantors, and there was no need under the contract to sue the debtor first. But it was felt to be morally wrong that he should sue a guarantor first–this can be seen as early as Cicero's day[13]–and eventually it was held that if he did, he would be liable on the *actio iniuriarum* brought by the debtor, since the creditor's behavior was treated as implying that the debtor was insolvent and not worth suing.

Other edicts soon followed. These covered public insult, certain attempts on the chastity of a Roman matron or a young man or woman, behavior aimed at making another legally disgraced, assaulting another's slave contrary to good morals primarily by beating him or having him tortured, *iniuriae* by a slave, and finally *iniuriae* to someone in power when the father or husband was away and had left no agent to act for him. These edicts were successful, and the actions given by the Twelve Tables ceased to be used. But, of course, they were not abolished, and later jurists continue to discuss them. In all the edictal actions a plaintiff who lost his case had to pay the defendant one tenth of his claim. Near the end of the Republic, Sulla issued a statute, the *lex Cornelia de iniuriis,* which gave something very close to a criminal action for striking, beating, or entering a house by force.

In addition to these four delicts which the *Institutes* might induce us to regard as the most important, there were a number of others.

About 80 B.C. a praetor, Octavius, issued an edict on extortion. One clause gave *restitutio in integrum;* that is, the innocent party was put into the position he would have been in but for the transaction; another gave an action *(actio quod metus causa)* for four times the loss. Either then or later a defense *(exceptio metus)* was given to the innocent party if the wrongdoer sued him on the contract.

10. *Noctes Atticae* 20.1.13.
11. Plautus *Asinaria* 371.
12. *Rhetorica ad Herennium* 2.13.19.
13. Cicero *Ad Atticum* 16.15.2.

In 66 B.C., Aquillius Gallus introduced his edict on fraud which gave both an action *(actio de dolo)* and a defense *(exceptio doli)*. The action gave the injured party only simple damages, and, moreover, he could bring the *actio de dolo* only if no other suitable action was available to him. This is different from other delictal actions and has seemed strange to many commentators, but the explanation lies in Aquillius's purpose. He said that a person was liable to the action "when one thing is pretended, another thing done."[14] Thus, the action was available only when there were dealings between the parties, and so it was really a contractual action. Hence, like other contractual actions its aim was to recompense one party for the loss suffered, not to penalize the other. Since the *actio de dolo* arose only when no other action was available, it had no place in any good faith contract and must have been intended for stipulation and the literal contract. Shortly after Aquillius's day the scope of the action was widened. Just at the beginning of the Empire, Labeo redefined fraud as "any stratagem, trick or machination used to circumvent, dupe or ensnare another."[15] Henceforth negotiations between the parties would not be necessary for the action.

The *exceptio doli* ran: "If in this matter nothing has been done or is being done fraudulently by the plaintiff." So the defense was available even when the fraud was not past fraud but lay in the very bringing of the action; we have a case of this kind when the judge was Aquillius Gallus himself.[16] A wealthy Roman, Gaius Visellius Varro, who thought he was dying, wanted to make a gift in the event of his death but only in that event *(donatio mortis causa)* to his mistress, Otacilia Laterensis. This could not be done directly, since such a gift would be void for immorality. So he gave Otacilia a stipulation for 300,000 *sesterces*. She recorded this in her account books as having been paid to her and made another entry that she had given Varro a loan of that sum. Thus a literal contract was made. Varro recovered, but Otacilia wanted the money and sued. Varro successfully defended, almost certainly by the *exceptio doli* and in virtue of the second part of it. Regret was expressed by the judge that Varro could not be both absolved from the plaintiff's claim and condemned.

Another edict gave an action for double damages *(actio servi corrupti)* against someone who took in another's runaway slave or fraudulently persuaded the slave to do something which made him worse. A slave could be made worse physically or morally, and the master's action

14. Cicero *De natura deorum* 3.30.74.
15. *Digest of Justinian* 4.3.1.2.
16. Valerius Maximus 8.2.2.

was understood to include the loss he suffered in any way, not just a fall
in the slave's market value. When a master who had freed the slave who
kept his accounts discovered afterwards that the slave had been embez-
zling his money to give to a "little woman," it was held that the action
should be available against the woman for the master's loss even though
the slave had been freed.[17] The praetor also provided for other situations
in his Edict, such as when a wife stole from her husband. It was felt to
be wrong that a husband should be able to sue his wife for theft so a
special action *(actio rerum amotarum)* was invented.

Some relatively minor delicts which were made actionable by the
Twelve Tables continued to exist in much later times. The action for
inserted material *(actio de tigno iniuncto)* was given for double damages
when stolen material was built into a house or used for supporting vines.
Wrongful cutting down of another's trees gave an *actio de arboribus
succisis.* The action for pasturing *(actio de pastu)* lay when someone sent
in his animals to feed on another's acorns. Still other actions were given
for dedicating to the gods property over which there was a legal dispute,
or for burning a house or heap of grain stored near a house.

QUASI DELICTS

Justinian classifies four obligations as arising *as if* from a delict.[18]
Gaius does not mention them in his *Institutes,* but texts from the *Digest*
suggest that the classification does go back to him.[19] Exactly why they
are regarded as distinct from ordinary delicts is a matter of great dispute.
When a judge "makes a law suit his own" *(judex qui litem suam fecerit),*
he is liable. Despite many ingenious answers it is still not known what
this wrong entailed. Under an edict, a person from whose dwelling
something was poured or thrown so that it caused an injury had to face
an action *(actio de effusis vel dejectis).* Whether he had thrown it or not,
or even knew about it, was irrelevant. Another edict gave an action
against a person who allowed something to be placed on or suspended
from the eaves or a projecting roof from which its fall could cause injury
(actio de suspensis). This time the inhabitant had to know that the thing
had been placed there, though he would be liable even if he had not done
the placing. The remaining quasi delict gave an action against a ship's
captain, innkeeper, or stablekeeper for any fraud or theft committed on
the ship or in the inn or stable by one of his workers. Some of the quasi
delicts are akin to modern vicarious liability, when one person is made

17. *Digest of Justinian* 11.3.16.
18. *Institutes of Justinian* 4.5.
19. *Digest of Justinian* 44.7.5.4, 5, 6 (Gaius *3 aureorum*).

liable for acts of his employees or other dependants even though he was unaware of what they were doing.

NOXAL LIABILITY

It was felt to be wrong that a father or master should suffer great loss if his son or slave committed a delict, hence from the earliest times it was possible for the father or master to restrict his loss to the worth of the son or slave. When a delictal action was brought against a paterfamilias for a wrong committed by a son or slave, he had the choice either of paying the amount of the claim or of handing over his dependent. If the master himself had also been involved in the wrong he usually lost his right to noxal surrender. In Justinian's time slaves alone could be noxally surrendered.

LIABILITY FOR ANIMALS.

The Twelve Tables gave an action against the owner of an animal which did damage for the amount of the loss or for the surrender of the animal *(actio de pauperie)*. The action was much discussed in late republican times, and the general opinion was that the action could only be given when the animal was at "fault," because it was vicious or, for instance, had taken fright; but it would not lie when the animal had been hurt or teased by someone. Quintus Mucius wrote that when rams or bulls fought and one killed the other, the action would not be allowed when the dead animal was the aggressor, but otherwise the owner of the aggressor would have to pay for the loss or surrender his animal.

The aediles–the magistrates in charge of the streets and marketplaces at Rome–issued an edict which gave an action if a wild animal which was kept near a road–usually, presumably, in readiness for a gladiatorial show–escaped and did damage. The action gave double damages for injury to *property,* the assessment was up to the judge if a free man was *injured,* and there was a fixed penalty of 200 *solidi* for the *death* of a free man.

IX

SUCCESSION

Succession on death could be under a will or on intestacy. Wills were recognized as early as the Twelve Tables; the two oldest types were *testamentum comitiis calatis* and the *testamentum in procinctu* (in battle order).

The first of these was made in the *comitia calata* which met twice a year, on March 24 and May 24, for the purpose of making wills. It seems, like *adrogatio,* to have been a legislative act, and it required the assent of the people. Its disadvantages are obvious–it is public, it requires popular approval, and it can be made only on two days a year–so that its early disappearance is not surprising.

The *testamentum in procinctu* was made when the army was drawn up in battle order after the auspices–that is, the ceremony to establish whether the omens for victory were favorable–had been taken. It needed no writing or other formalities; it died out, however, sometime after the middle of the second century B.C., and before the time of Cicero, because as a result of political changes the military commander began to wage war only after he had laid aside his power (as an ex-magistrate) of taking auspices. In classical law there was another military will which required no formalities, one which was first introduced by Julius Caesar. It existed at that time for only a short period but was later reintroduced.

A third form *(testamentum per aes et libram)*–historically much more important–was not in the Twelve Tables but emerged early as another adaptation of *mancipatio*. As a *mancipatio* it required the five witnesses, the scale-holder, and a person to whom the estate was transferred *(familiae emptor)*. The *familiae emptor* said: "I declare that your belongings and money are in my care and custody so that you can make a valid will according to the public statute, and let them have been bought by me with this bronze and by these bronze scales." He struck the scales with the piece of bronze, which he gave to the testator as the

84

symbolic price. The testator then said: "As it is written on these wax tablets, so I give, so I legate, so I declare in my will; and you, citizens, bear me witness." This second declaration *(nuncupatio)* confirmed the provisions which were written on the tablets, but in fact it was not necessary for the provisions to be written down at all, and the testator could declare orally the terms of the will. Originally, the testator's property would pass at once to the *familiae emptor,* who was only under a moral duty to fulfill the conditions of the will. In classical law, the *familiae emptor* had become a mere figurehead and was totally unimportant; the testator remained the owner of the property until he died. This was the standard will of the late Republic and Empire. In practice the written document would be sealed with the seals of the five witnesses to the *mancipatio,* the scale-holder, and the *familiae emptor.* A great boost was given to this practice by a praetor's edict, in existence in Cicero's time,[1] which declared that if there was a dispute over an inheritance and written tablets were produced, sealed with the requisite number of seals, the praetor would give the person named as heir the possession of the property. The validity of the will could, of course, still be disputed, but the heir named in the written will was put in the strongest position from the start.

Other forms of will were introduced in late law. The main one is the tripartite will–so called because it derives from three sources–introduced in 439 A.D.[2] This had to be made in one operation and before seven witnesses (which were civil law requirements), the witnesses had to seal (which was a praetorian requirement), and the testator had to sign (which was an imperial innovation). This became the ordinary will of late Roman law.

A will could be made only by a sane Roman citizen above the age of puberty who was not in *patriapotestas.* Until the time of Hadrian a woman who was not in power could make a will only if she had undergone a change of family (e.g., by having been married *cum manu)* after becoming free of *patriapotestas.* Both before and after Hadrian, a woman who could make a will must still have the consent of her tutor.

A will to be effective in any way whatever must designate an heir who was both properly appointed and properly qualified and who accepted the inheritance. Only a Roman could be appointed heir with the sole exception that slaves, whether of the testator or of another Roman, were eligible. A slave of the testator could only be appointed heir if he was

1. Cicero *In Verrem* 2.1.45.117, though the form of the clause is significantly different from what it was later.
2. *Code of Justinian* 6.23.21.

also given his freedom in the will, though, in Justinian's time at least, the appointment as heir would in itself act as a gift of liberty. When another's slave was appointed heir, the slave became heir but all the property would go to his master. Unborn descendants could be appointed heir— and indeed if a *suus heres* came into being after the will was made, and no provision had been made for him, the will was void. The antifeminist *lex Voconia* of 169 B.C. laid down, among other things, that a person in the first class of the census, the wealthiest class, could not appoint a woman as his heir. This applied even if his sole child was a daughter,[3] but the provision lost its significance in the early Empire because of the introduction of trusts *(fideicommissa)*.

The institution of an heir had to be in the proper form, either "Let Titius be my heir" or "I order Titius to be my heir." Any other form of words was ineffective. This was the most important part of the will; anything written in front of the institution of the heir was ignored. Heirs fell into three types, *necessarii, sui et necessarii,* and *extranei.* Necessary heirs *(necessarii)* were the testator's slaves, and they could not refuse the inheritance. *Sui et necessarii* were those persons who were in the testator's power and became independent on his death (thus, it did not include those grandchildren who fell into the power of their father when the grandfather died). At first they, too, could not refuse the inheritance, but later they were given relief. *Extranei* were outsiders and they could refuse the inheritance. The significance of this is that, contrary to modern law, a Roman heir was liable for all the debts of the deceased even when they exceeded the assets. It frequently happened that a person named as heir refused the inheritance or died before the testator. To combat the danger that there would be no heir it was normal to appoint a number of subsequent heirs *(substituti)* who would take the inheritance if those previously named refused to do so or had died. Often such a list of heirs would close with one of the testator's slaves, who could not refuse the inheritance. If debts were greater than assets, it was the slave, now free, who would be declared insolvent and suffer disgrace, not the dead testator. All *sui,* including those born after the will was made, had to be either nominated testamentary heir or disinherited; in general sons had to be expressly disinherited, daughters and remoter descendants could be disinherited by a general clause, such as "Let all others be disinherited." A close relative who was disinherited without good reason might bring an action to have the will set aside as undutiful *(querella inofficiosi testamenti).*

3. Cicero *De finibus* 2.17.55; Saint Augustine *De civitate Dei* 3.21.

A special type of substitution of heirs was that called pupillary substitution *(substitutio pupillaris)*. If a father appointed as his heir one of his *sui* who was still under puberty, he could appoint a substitute in case the child died after he had become heir but before he reached puberty. The substitute in effect would be succeeding to the child (who, of course, could not himself make a will) under the father's will. In ordinary substitution *(substitutio vulgaris)* the substitute became heir only if the person previously named as heir did not become heir at all. There was a famous case between 93 and 91 B.C. on the interpretation of a clause of substitution.[4] The testator had no son, but he did have hopes of one when he made his will, and the clause of substitution ran: "Let X be my heir if my son dies before he reaches puberty." The testator died leaving no son, and a dispute arose between the substituted heir and those who would be the heirs if the will did not come into effect. Quintus Mucius Scaevola appeared for the heirs on intestacy and argued that the wording showed that the clause was only a clause of pupillary substitution, not a clause of ordinary substitution, and hence could operate only if a son had actually been born to the testator and had died after the testator but before reaching puberty. The famous orator Lucius Crassus appeared for the substitute and argued that the intention of the testator was what was most important; that the testator's intention certainly was that the substitute should be heir if no son of the testator reached puberty, whether one had been born or not; and hence that a clause of pupillary substitution carried within it a clause of ordinary substitution. Crassus won.

Wills could contain clauses other than the appointment of heirs; the most important were those for the manumission of slaves,[5] the appointment of tutors to infants,[6] legacies, and trusts *(fideicommissa)*.

A legacy was a gift left by will which was payable by the heir alone. In classical law there were four kinds. A legacy by a claim of ownership *(per vindicationem)* occurred when the testator expressed himself in formal words as making the gift to the legatee. Basically the legatee became owner of the thing as soon as the will was effective, and hence this kind of legacy could only be used for things which had been owned by the testator. There was a legacy *per damnationem* when the testator ordered the heir, again in formal words, to give the legacy to the legatee. This gave the legatee the right to a personal action against the heir, and if the heir unsuccessfully defended he was condemned in a sum twice the value of the legacy. Of little importance was the legacy *sinendi modo*,

---

4. Cicero *De oratore* 1.39.180; *De inventione* 2.42.122; *Brutus* 52-53.194-198.

5. See above, pp. 46f.

6. See above, chapter 4, under Tutelage.

by sufferance. Here the heir was ordered to allow the legatee to take the thing. This also gave the legatee a personal action against the heir, but if the heir lost he had only to give the value. Last there was the legacy *per praeceptionem,* by taking first. This was used when an estate was left to more than one heir, and one (or more) of the heirs was given a legacy which he was to take before the estate was divided. The most common case would be when a father left his estate equally among his children but gave each a legacy *per praeceptionem* of his *peculium.* Only a Roman citizen could be left a legacy. The rules of legacy were simplified by the *senatusconsultum Neronianum* of 64 A.D., which said that if a legacy was made in a form not appropriate to it, it should be treated as a legacy made in the form best suited to give it effect, *per damnationem.* By Justinian's time there was no longer any need for formal words for legacies.

Trusts *(fideicommissa)* occurred in the Republic, but they had only moral force. Augustus enforced them in a few individual instances, and they were soon fully regarded as binding. They were mainly useful for avoiding the restrictions on the institution of heirs and, to a lesser extent, on legacies. Thus, the *lex Voconia* of 169 B.C., which had forbidden very rich persons from appointing women as their heirs, could be circumvented by the testator's appointing a male heir and then directing him by way of trust to give the whole estate to a woman. There were very few legal restrictions on trusts. Of course, it could happen that the person named as heir would not accept the inheritance because there was so little profit in it for him–the same might be true if much were left by legacy–and there was legislation to enable the named heir always to keep at least some part of the inheritance. Justinian enacted that there should be no distinction between legacies and trusts and that each should have the advantages of the other.[7]

Codicils, informal additions to wills, were made enforceable by Augustus. He and others had been appointed heirs by a wealthy man called Lentulus who imposed trusts on the heirs in a codicil. Augustus ordered the trusts to be carried out and then asked legal advice on whether codicils should be made legally enforceable. The answer was that they should.

INTESTATE SUCCESSION

When there was no will–or no effective will–the property was divided according to certain rules. The law of intestate succession is a mass of detail which underwent continual change and which need not concern

7. *Code of Justinian* 6.43.1; *Institutes of Justinian* 2.20.3.

us here. The system of the Twelve Tables rested completely on agnation, that is, relationship through males.[8] This was gradually altered, at first by the praetor's Edict and then by imperial legislation from the time of Hadrian. After Justinian's legislation in his *Novels* the old civil law rules had completely disappeared, and intestate succession was primarily based on blood relationship. It is, though, of particular significance that at no time was the eldest born given greater rights than other *sui* in the same degree of relationship. Males and females were likewise treated alike until after the *lex Voconia* in the Republic, when it was held that no woman except a sister could succeed on intestacy as an agnate.

8. Except that patrons had certain rights to the inheritance of their freedmen.

X

POSTCLASSICAL LAW AND JUSTINIAN

SHORTLY AFTER the murder of Ulpian in 228 A.D. by the Praetorian Guard, Roman law went into decline, and no new jurists of note were forthcoming. The center of empire moved from Rome to the Greek East, where intellectual traditions were different and law did not have the same fascination. Besides, when the Empire became Christian in 325 A.D., theology became the study most attractive to those with leisure.

This postclassical period, as it is called, is most marked by the effort to keep what had previously been gained, not by any attempt to make further progress. The law books which we know of for the period fall primarily into two classes. Some are collections or anthologies of earlier texts, illustrating the law on certain topics. The *Vatican Fragments (Fragmenta Vaticana),* which must date from after 382 A.D., contain texts from the classical jurists, Papinian, Paul, and Ulpian, and a number of statutes. *The Comparison of Mosaic and Roman Laws (Collatio legum Mosaicarum et Romanarum)* is to be dated between 390 and 438, but it seems also to have had an earlier form. It gives side by side provisions of biblical law and Roman law. The purpose of the original author–it is disputed whether he is Christian or Jew–is uncertain, but the work is probably an attempt to show that Mosaic law had earlier reached all the essential conclusions of Roman law. The other important class of books consists of teaching works, and they are in the main abridgments of classical elementary textbooks. Examples of such works are the *Epitome of Ulpian (Ulpiani Epitome),* the *Autun Gaius* which is a simplified version of Gaius's *Institutes,* and the *Opinions of Paul (Pauli Sententiae),* a collection made from the writings of that jurist.

During this period the works of five classical jurists, Ulpian, Paul, Papinian, Modestinus, and Gaius, began to have overwhelming popularity. It was only at this time that Gaius was accorded the importance which since has been regarded as his due. Legislation emphasized the importance of these writers; such laws reached their culmination in

90

the famous Law of Citations of Theodosius II in 426 A.D.[1] All the writings of these five jurists were made authoritative, and Gaius was expressly said to have the same authority as the other four. The writings of jurists cited by any of the five were also declared to have weight, but their opinions had to be checked by collation of manuscripts. When the five expressed conflicting opinions, the view of the majority was to prevail; if they were equally divided (for instance if one had not expressed an opinion), the view of the side on which Papinian stood was to be preferred; when they were equally divided and no opinion of Papinian was known, the judge could follow the side he preferred. This Law of Citations marks a low point of Roman jurisprudence, since the correct opinion is to be found by counting heads, not by choosing the best solution. But things were not so bad as is sometimes thought. The possibility of future development was not excluded, at least not for new situations or when the law had been or would be changed by legislation. Indeed, the Law of Citations compares favorably with the modern strict doctrine of precedent in Anglo-American law under which a court is bound by a decision of a higher court, regardless of whether at that time the court was composed of undistinguished men or had reached its decision by illogical arguments. The Law of Citations had at least the merit of singling out the best jurists to be followed.

The emperors continued to legislate, but the scarcity of able jurists heightened a problem which had already existed in classical law, that of ensuring that lawyers knew of the existence of the relevant legislation. To remedy this, two unofficial collections of imperial constitutions were issued, the *Codex Gregorianus* in 291 and the *Codex Hermogenianus* in 295. Neither has survived. In 438 was published the *Codex Theodosianus,* which was an official collection made on the instructions of the Emperor Theodosius II. Theodosius had appointed a nine-man commission in 429, with instructions to compile a collection of all the statutes since the time of Constantine which had been meant to be of general application. When this was completed, the compilers were to extract from it and from the *Codices Gregorianus* and *Hermogenianus* and the writings of the jurists all that was still useful and not obsolete, and this second collection was to be given statutory effect. The scheme was overambitious and was dropped, but in 435 a new commission, this time of sixteen men, was set up, with the more limited aim of collecting all the general imperial constitutions, but with power to alter them to bring them up to date. This commission completed its task in two years.

1. *Codex Theodosianus* 1.4.3.

Despite the vicissitudes which Roman law had suffered since the classical period, it was in the sixth century A.D. to be put into a new format, by the Emperor Justinian, which would make it the most fruitful source of law the world has ever known. Justinian was born of peasant stock in Serbia and was adopted by his uncle, Justin, who rose from the ranks to be proclaimed emperor in 518. Justinian even then had considerable influence on his uncle, and in 527 he was given joint control of the Empire. When Justin died later in the same year, Justinian became sole emperor and at once began the task of restating the law.

At the beginning of 528 he set up a ten-man commission which included Tribonian, his right-hand man, and Theophilus, a law professor at Constantinople. Their task was to prepare a new collection of imperial enactments drawn from the three previous codes and later constitutions. They were given wide powers: all that was unnecessary or out of date was to be omitted, and alterations could be made in the constitutions to bring them up to date. Fourteen months later this *Code* was published. It remained in force until 534 and has not survived.

Justinian next set about dealing with juristic writings. Here there was no earlier model such as had been available for the *Code.* The mass of material was also far greater, and there was probably more divergence of views among the jurists than was to be found in the constitutions. To settle some of the problems outstanding in the writings of the jurists, Justinian issued a number of constitutions, and a collection of the most important, known as the *Fifty Decisions (Quinquaginta Decisiones),* was made. This collection, too, is lost.

Justinian was now in a position to begin his codification of juristic writings. In a constitution of December 15, 530, he gave instructions to Tribonian. Tribonian was to choose a commission, and he appointed sixteen men including the great professors, Theophilus and Dorotheus. They were to make excerpts from the ancient writers of authority. There is no reason to see in this wording of the constitution a reference to the ancient *ius respondendi.* The excerpts were to be grouped according to subject matter in fifty books, and the books were further to be divided into titles. The commission was given full and unhampered power to choose the best view on each point and was instructed to cut out all dissensions and all that was obsolete or superfluous. Nothing which was already in the *Code* was to be included. This last point shows that Justinian's aim was not to change and modernize the writings of the classical jurists. They were not to be brought up to date–later alterations in law were the work of subsequent emperors, and their constitutions, so far as acceptable, were in the *Code.* But what was inconsistent with

Justinian's law was simply to be left out. The commission, in fact, was so concerned with the value of the original work that in each title the individual excerpts from the jurists begin with the name of the jurist, the name of the book, and the volume number from which the excerpt is taken. Ulpian was the most popular jurist, and about one half of the *Digest* comes from him. Paul ranks next with one sixth. According to Justinian almost 2,000 books containing 3,000,000 lines were read, and these were reduced to 150,000 lines. The finished work, known as the *Digest* or *Pandects,* was issued in 533. With the haste shown by the compilers it is inevitable that the work contains defects: above all, many of the contradictory opinions of the jurists remain. But the great unwieldy mass of classical juristic writing was reduced to an authoritative and manageable whole. To keep it this way, Justinian had already forbidden commentaries, and only translations into Greek were permitted. Whatever criticisms of the work can be made, the use made of the *Digest* in later ages shows that the compilers succeeded admirably in the main task.

Before the *Digest* was completed, Justinian issued instructions for the production of a new elementary textbook, the *Institutes.* The task was entrusted to Tribonian, Theophilus, and Dorotheus; it is probable that Tribonian acted only as overseer, that one portion was the sole work of Theophilus, the other of Dorotheus. The compilers were told to base their work on the elementary writings of the classical jurists, especially those of Gaius, and they followed the instructions closely. The basic pattern of the work is that of Gaius's *Institutes:* the topics follow in the same order; both works are in four books; but, unlike Gaius's *Institutes,* those of Justinian have each book subdivided into titles. The *Institutes* were published late in 533, they were given the force of statute, and they came into effect on December 30, 533, the same day as the *Digest.*

Many constitutions had been issued since 529 so Justinian, to make his codification complete, gave instructions for the compilation of a new collection of imperial constitutions. This second *Code (codex repetitae praelectionis)* was issued in 534 and, like the *Digest* and *Institutes,* has survived. It also is divided into books and titles according to subject matter. In each title the constitutions are given in chronological order.

Though this second *Code* brought the work of codification to an end, Justinian found it necessary to continue to legislate on many matters. His later legislation, the *New Constitutions (novellae constitutiones)* or *Novels,* has also survived; these four works, the *Digest, Institutes,* second *Code,* and the *Novels,* form what is now usually called the *Corpus Juris Civilis.*

XI

THE SUBSEQUENT HISTORY OF ROMAN LAW

MODERN SCHOLARS frequently talk of the "second life of Roman law." The expression is inexact and unjust. Roman law reappeared in so many ways at so many times in so many places that one would properly have to speak of "lives."

The first acceptance of Roman law in territory which was not controlled by the Romans occurred as early as the beginning of the sixth century A.D. The Roman Empire in the West ended in 476–the traditional date for the beginning of the Middle Ages–when the Emperor Romulus Augustulus was dethroned. Even before that date much of it had been overrun by the barbarian tribes, such as the Visigoths and the Burgundians. The Visigoths established themselves in Spain and southwestern France, and in 506 their king Alaric II enacted the *Lex Romana Visigothorum,* a compilation of law for his Roman subjects. It contains extracts from the *Codex Theodosianus* and post-Theodosian *Novels,* from the *Codex Gregorianus* and the *Codex Hermogenianus,* an epitome of Gaius's *Institutes,* a selection from Paul's *Opinions* and one *responsum* of the jurist Papinian. All the texts, except for the epitome of Gaius, are accompanied by an explanatory paraphrase called an *interpretatio.* The object of the compilation was the same as that of Justinian's later codification. Recceswind repealed the code in 654 A.D. and issued the *Lex Visigothorum Recesvindiana,* which was to apply equally to Romans and Visigoths. The *Lex Romana Visigothorum* was, it seems, virtually forgotten in Spain. But it remained alive in France where, indeed, it was the main instrument of the survival of Roman law in the West until the revival of Roman law in the eleventh century.

A second compilation was enacted at the beginning of the sixth century A.D. by the Burgundians, probably under King Gundobad, for their Roman subjects. This, the *Lex Romana Burgundionum,* consists not of extracts from Roman works but of statements of legal rules. Of lesser importance is the *Edictum Theoderici* issued between 493 and 507 by the king of the Ostrogoths.

94

The main vehicle, however, for the dissemination of Roman law was Justinian's codification, which was influential in both the East and the West. The emperor, who wished his work to remain in force forever, had forbidden commentaries and allowed only translations into Greek and synopses *(indices)*. But in the East even in his own lifetime his prohibition was not obeyed.

Theophilus, one of the main compilers of both the *Digest* and the *Institutes*. composed a very much larger rendering of the *Institutes* into Greek which is known as the *Paraphrase.* Dorotheus, an almost equally important compiler, wrote an *index* to the *Digest.* Two others of the compilers, Thaleaeus and Isidorus, wrote works on the *Code.* Later, at the end of the sixth or beginning of the seventh century an unknown jurist–universally called Anonymous–made one large work out of earlier commentaries on the *Digest.* This had the form of a "chain" commentary, a form also found in Byzantine theological works.

Not long after this a new drop in legal standards meant that the *Corpus Juris* could not be properly used, and led eventually to the publication about 740 A.D. of a new work called the *Ecloga.* This was the first official Byzantine codification; it was issued under Leo the Isaurian (who was the first Iconoclast emperor) and his son Constantine Copronimus. It is based primarily on Justinian's *Institutes,* but also upon his *Code, Digest,* and *Novels,* and upon non-Roman sources. Scripture is cited as authority for legal rules. Throughout the eighteen titles there is a strong emphasis on justice, humanitarian principles, and Christian ethics. Shortly afterwards three minor collections were made on maritime, agrarian, and military law, but there was then little legal activity for the next hundred years.

Revitalization came with the accession of the Emperor Basil I (867-886), the founder of the Macedonian dynasty. About 879 he published the *Procheiron,* a manual in forty books intended to take the place of the *Ecloga,* which was considered heretical. It dealt mainly with the law of persons and succession. The *Procheiron* was of very considerable influence – especially, because of its subject matter, in ecclesiastical courts– and was even translated into Arabic in the thirteenth century. A revised version, known as the *Epanoge,* was published about 885. But Basil's main claim to fame among lawyers is that he was the instigator of the great compilation, now known as the *Basilica,* which was issued under his son, Leo III. This is in sixty books which are divided into titles; within each title are collected the relevant parts (with some changes) of Justinian's *Digest, Code,* and *Novels,* and sometimes of the *Institutes.* The work is completely in Greek, and was prepared from the Greek works which followed Justinian in the sixth and seventh centuries. Official *scholia* were soon added to it and so, later, were unofficial *scholia*. How influential it was and how widely it was used is a matter of debate among scholars, but it is known that even after the fall of Constantinople in 1453 it was in force in the Byzantine churches.

After the *Basilica* no new work of great importance was issued in the East, but various epitomes emerged. These culminated about 1345 in the *Hexabiblos,* which was the work of Harmenopulos, a judge in Salonica. This was based on the *Ecloga* and other works, hence its description as "a miserable epitome of epitomes of epitomes." By a decree of 1835, the *Hexabiblos* was declared to be in force in Greece, subject to contrary custom and court practice, until a civil code could be issued. The Greek Civil Code, however, did not come into force until February 23, 1946, and till then the *Hexabiblos* was the law of the land. The Greek civil courts before 1946 relied very heavily on the work of the (German) Pandect writers (to be discussed shortly), and the Civil Code itself is strongly influenced by German legal science.

In the West the survival of Roman law was for a long time far less secure. After a war which lasted eighteen years, Justinian brought Italy under Byzantine rule in 553, and in 554 Justinian's codification was imposed on Italy by a statute known as the *Sanctio pragmatica pro petitione Vigilii.* It is doubtful how far the codification was used in the conditions then prevailing in Italy, and in 568 the Lombards gained control of all except Ravenna, southern Italy, and Sicily. In these areas still under Byzantine control standards remained fairly high, thanks above all to the monasteries, and the law was applied territorially, that is, to everyone in the region no matter what his personal origins. Elsewhere in the West standards were very low, and personal law applied–the law which ruled a person was that of his own people, irrespective of where he might be. As an example of the standards prevailing in the Lombard period I might cite *liber* 1.4 of the eighth-century *Lex Romana Raetica Curiensis,* which was intended for the Roman people of eastern Switzerland and was also used in the Tyrol and northern Italy. *Liber* 1.4 seeks to establish the use of the Law of Citations. Papinian appears, not for the first time, as Papian, Gaius as Gagius, and Scaevola as Scifola. Stranger still, the law is taken to mean that each party to a lawsuit should produce supporters, and he who has more supporters is to win. If the number of supporters is equal, that party is to win whose claim is backed by an opinion of Papian. The system of personal law added greatly to the confusion. Agobard, Bishop of Lyons about 850, said it frequently happened that of five persons who were together each was governed by a different law. But the personal law of the Church in the West was Roman, and hence a considerable amount of Roman law was incorporated into canon law. The system of personal law was so inconvenient that it was gradually abandoned in favor of territorial law, and thereafter Roman law as a system was no longer anywhere in force in the West.

The revival began in Bologna in the late eleventh century. Tradition ascribes the first teaching of Roman law to a *legis doctor* called Pepo, who is mentioned in a judgment of 1076 in which the *Digest* is quoted. Official teaching of Roman law seems, however, to have begun at the beginning of the next century with Irnerius, also in Bologna, and Bologna became a center of legal studies to which students flocked from all over Western Europe. The personal genius of Irnerius in mastering and communicating the new science should not be underestimated, but it must also be stressed that better economic and social circumstances provided conditions in which Roman law could be properly utilized. The rediscovery of the *Digest* sometime before the middle of the eleventh century also played a vital role. Irnerius was succeeded by four of his pupils, Bulgarus, Martinus, Jacobus, and Ugo, who are known as "the four doctors."

Irnerius and his school are known as the Glossators because their main literary form was the gloss, that is, a comment or commentary on a word, phrase, or text, inserted into the manuscript of the original work. If the comment was short—for instance a single cross-reference—it would be inserted above the relevant line, if it was longer it would be written in the margin. As these glosses increased in number the original text began to occupy a relatively small space in the middle of the page. The influence of the Glossators before the middle of the twelfth century was enormous even outside Italy. Thus, Vacarius, one of their number, was the first to teach Roman law in England, at Oxford before 1250. He was brought over, probably at the instigation of the future archbishop, Thomas à Becket, who had himself studied law at Bologna. Vacarius's most famous work, the *Liber pauperum (The Book of the Poor Students),* which has survived, is a condensed version of Justinian's *Code* with contributions from the *Digest.* His lectures on Justinian's *Institutes,* and some other works by him, have recently come to light but are not yet published. And in France, a summary of Justinian's *Code, Lo Codi,* written in Provençal at Arles about 1149, displays very clearly its dependence on the works of the Glossators.

No extensive work of the first Glossators has survived. The earliest work by a known author is the *Summa Codicis,* which was written by

Rogerius, a pupil of Bulgarus. But there exist a number of other works from this time that give us a good idea what their work was like.

The two most celebrated Glossators of the first half of the thirteenth century are Azo and Accursius. Azo's commentaries on the *Code* and *Institutes*, the *Summa Codicis* and the *Summa Institutionum*, were for centuries regarded as the best introduction to Roman law. Accursius is perhaps even better known. He collected previous glosses, selected the most important, and reconciled differing interpretations so successfully that his resulting work was written into all subsequent manuscripts of the *Corpus Juris Civilis* which were copied at Bologna. This Accursian gloss is usually called the *glossa ordinaria.*

The most significant centers of Roman legal study in the second half of the thirteenth century were not in Italy but in France, and especially at Orleans and Toulouse. The teachers, at least of the first generation, had themselves studied at Bologna, but their works are distinguished by a greater interest in legal history. Their most famous scholars were Jacobus de Raveneio and Petrus de Bellapertica. But by the early fourteenth century Italy had regained the mastery under Cinus de Pistorio, who was greatly influenced by the French and may even have been a pupil of Bellapertica. His pupil, Bartolus de Saxoferrato, was the most influential of all the medieval jurists, and his numerous works are found in a great many manuscripts. What is called the "Reception of Roman Law" owes a very great deal to him and his pupil, Baldus de Ubaldis.

The story of that "Reception"–that is, the assimilation of the learned Roman law as taught at the universities into the law of the individual territories of Western Europe–is complex and as yet not fully understood. But in general it can be said that the successful graduate, appointed as an ecclesiastical or secular administrator, or acting as a judge or advocate, was not content to allow decisions to be reached on the basis of the inferior native law. Roman legal ways of thinking began to creep into the native law, so that throughout Western Europe (apart from the British Isles and Scandinavia), jurists of different territories had a similar approach to law. Especially in those territories where the administration of the law was backward, Roman law came to be accepted as the law of the land.

In the south of France, for instance, the Reception is shown first in the use of Roman legal terminology, which, together with the ever increasing expertise in Roman law, led eventually to the acceptance in practice of particular Roman rules. To withstand the penetration of Roman law many Midi towns issued codes of their legal customs, but some of the codes actually contained a considerable amount of Roman law. In the thirteenth century the influence of Roman law there was even greater, thanks to those who had studied at Orleans, Toulouse, and Montpellier. The process was concluded when in the sixteenth century the upper courts habitually applied Roman law.

The main vehicle of the Reception in Spain was the systematic and comprehensive *Codigo de las Siete Partidas* which was composed in the middle of the thirteenth century by a number of jurists, probably at the instigation of Alfonso X of Castile. Its sources were the customs of Castile and Leon, canon law, and Justinian's *Digest* (plus Italian juristic writing on it); the last two sources predominated. It did not at first have the force of law, but its influence continually grew, and it was given full legal effect in 1348. The *Siete Partidas,* later Spanish enactments, and the legal digest of 1567 known as the *Nueva Recõpilaciõn* were to be of fundamental importance in bringing Roman law to the Spanish territories in the New World.

The Reception in Germany occurred later, primarily in the fifteenth and sixteenth centuries, and it was more complete. The political division into over three hundred separate and independent territories, though all were under the Holy Roman emperor, meant that very many were administratively backward and presented ideal conditions for the acceptance of a more developed system. The process of the Reception was greatly helped when the supreme court of the Holy Roman Empire, the *Reichskammergericht,* was remodeled in 1495, and it was laid down that half of the court were to be *Doctores iuris,* that is, jurists trained in Roman law. Local rulers followed this example.

In Scotland the Reception was later still. Legal studies at the Scottish universities were primitive, when they existed at all, and the enmity of England closed Oxford and Cambridge to the Scots. Until the sixteenth century many Scots studied law in France, and after the Reformation in Holland. There they imbibed Roman law, which inevitably influenced their approach on their return home. In 1681 Lord Stair first published his great work, *The Institutions of the Law of Scotland,* which was an enormous success and formed the basis of modern Scots law.

Before this, however, the spirit of the Renaissance had influenced a new breed of humanist jurists. They were no longer content to use the *Corpus Juris Civilis* for the needs of their own society but sought the original Roman sense. At the beginning of this movement in the early sixteenth century stand the Italian, Alciatus, and the German, Zasius. Another German, Haloander, was the first to edit Justinian's Greek *Novels,* in his famous edition of the *Corpus Juris Civilis* which was published between 1529 and 1531. But the most famous humanists were

French, especially Cuiacius and Donellus. Cuiacius's chief work is his twenty-eight books of *Observationes et Emendationes*. These comments and emendations were on Greek and Latin literary texts as well as on legal works, and, as a true humanist, his legal interests were not confined to the law of Justinian. For instance, he wrote a treatise on Africanus, commentaries on Papinian, edited–and saved for posterity–pre-Justinianic works including part of the *Theodosian Code*. He also procured, though he himself did not publish, the manuscript of the *Basilica*. Donellus's main writings were on succession, escheat, and on titles of the *Digest* and *Code*.

Some of the French humanists, including Donellus, were Huguenots and were forced to emigrate when persecution began in 1573. In Holland they were especially influential, and it is in part due to them that in the seventeenth century the Netherlands was the scene of the greatest juristic production. The great Dutch jurists of the seventeenth and early eighteenth century display a remarkable diversity of approach. The earliest, and perhaps most influential of all, was Grotius. He wrote his *Inleiding tot de Hollandsche Rechtsgeleertheyd (Introduction to the Jurisprudence of Holland)* between 1619 and 1621 when he was in prison for political offenses. In this work he treated the law of Holland–which was heavily influenced by Roman law–as a system on its own, with pure Roman law very much in the background.[1] Groenewegen published his *Tractatus de legibus abrogatis et inusitatis in Hollandia vicinisque regionibus (Treatise on the Laws Abrogated and in Desuetude in Holland and Neighbouring Regions)* in 1649. This is a systematic account of the rules and laws which appear in Justinian but which were no longer in use in Holland. His debt to Grotius is shown in that he annotated that jurist's *Inleiding*. Of a very different type was Noodt who published a commentary on the first twenty-seven books of the *Digest* in 1713 and who wrote treatises on the *lex Aquilia,* usufruct, and pacts. He was concerned to recover pure Roman law. Between the two extremes stands Voet, whose main work, the *Commentarius ad Pandectas (Commentary on the Digest)* was published in two volumes, the first in 1698, the second in 1704. He gives both the Roman and the contemporary law. His influence has been enormous, not only because of the quality of his opinions but also because in a relatively short compass he gives a comprehensive account of the law.

During the sixteenth century individual jurists demanded a codifica-

1. Outside the Netherlands and South Africa, Grotius is more remembered for his classic work on international law, *De iure belli ac pacis (The Law of War and Peace).*

tion of the law to solve the ever-growing problems of complexity and uncertainty. To a very considerable degree this desire for a code was itself due to the example of the *Corpus Juris Civilis,* but it must be admitted that the jurists in part wished to restrain the influence of Roman law. Thus in the second half of the sixteenth century Francis Hotman in France favored a code drawn partly from Roman law, partly from the writings of philosophers, court practice, and the Bible. The famous German philosopher, Leibnitz, suggested that a companion code to Justinian's *Corpus Juris* be made, in order to bring it up to date. The first modern attempt at official codification–the origins can be traced to 1738 though the code was not published until 1794–was Prussia's *Allegemeines Landrecht für die preussischen Staaten.* This code, which was heavily influenced by the doctrines of natural law, had as one of its objects the restriction of Roman law,[2] though in fact much of it is Roman. In some ways natural law theories tended to strengthen the position of Roman law since to a great extent Justinian's *Corpus Juris* could be regarded as the "Law of Reason." It is above all this attitude which accounts for the influence of Roman law in the United States in the eighteenth and early nineteenth centuries.

Codification of law in Western Europe involved both a defeat and a victory for Roman law: defeat in that Roman law lost most of its power to develop further the law of a country adopting a codification (since practicing lawyers rarely look behind the code), but victory in that much Roman law is enshrined in the codes, and in that the codes themselves provide useful models for developing states in Asia and Africa.

The most important codes are France's *Code Napoleón* of 1804, the Austrian Code of 1811, and the *Bürgerliches Gesetzbuch* which became law throughout a politically united Germany in 1900. Of these the first and the last have been particularly influential. For instance, the codes of Spain and Ethiopia owe much to the French, those of Switzerland and Japan to the German.

One aspect of German legal development demands particular mention. In the nineteenth century, Germany became heavily industrialized, but in many of the states of that–as yet–not united country Roman law was the law of the land. To meet the needs of an industrial society, certain leading jurists were prepared to interpret the Roman sources in a very artifical way. The most influential of these jurists, who are now known as the Pandectists, was Windscheid.

2. The first section of the *Avis* of May 9, 1746, reads, "Above all, Roman Latin law should be abolished, and on Prussian soil a German territorial law developed, which must base itself solely on natural reason and the constitutions of the state."

Outside Europe the main territories which have a system largely based on, or derived from, Roman law are Louisiana,[3] the Philippines, Quebec, the countries of South America, Turkey, Japan, Siam, Ceylon, Egypt, Ethiopia, and South Africa.

In Scotland, South Africa, Louisiana, and Quebec, there is now also a strong admixture of English common law. Modern civil law systems, with the exception of South Africa and Scotland, are codified.

3. Considerable traces of Roman law can be found in other states, particularly in Texas and Arkansas.

APPENDIX

SELECTED TEXTS

THE MAIN SOURCES of our knowledge of Roman law are, of course, Justinian's *Corpus Juris Civilis* and Gaius's *Institutes.* But important information is also to be found in nonlegal works such as the writings of Cicero. In this appendix are collected a few texts of both sorts, arranged chronologically, which are thought to throw particular light on legal science.

1. Romulus, the founder of the city of Rome in 753 B.C., who is said to have separated the patricians and plebeians, allowed each plebeian to choose a patron from the patricians, and assigned rights and duties to each. Dionysius of Halicarnassus records thus the duties of the dependants:

> It was the duty of the *clientes* to help their patrons in providing dowries for their daughters if the fathers lacked funds; to redeem them from the enemy if they or their sons were captured; to pay on their behalf the sums awarded against them in private law suits and their fines if they were condemned in criminal trials.[1]

Dionysius then describes the duties common to both *clientes* and patrons. These duties that fell on *clientes* alone are remarkable. There is no trace of them for any later period of Roman law, and it is unlikely that they long survived, yet they correspond to a remarkable degree to certain aspects of casualties, incidents of medieval feudalism. One of the incidents of tenure by knight service was that the lord could demand a sum of money, called an aid, from his tenant in three circumstances: when the lord was imprisoned and needed a ransom, when he wished to make his eldest son a knight, and when he wished a dowry for the marriage of his eldest daughter. In a very real sense it is this correspondence–a coincidence not resulting from knowledge of Romulus's law but from social needs which were sufficiently similar–which justifies belief in the substantial accuracy of Dionysius' account.

1. *Antiquitates Romanae* 2.10.

2. The first–and for a very long time the only–codification of Roman law was the Twelve Tables of 451/450 B.C. The first table must have been concerned with procedure. We know this because Cicero writes: "When we were small, Quintus, we learnt 'if one summons another to court' "[2] and he is clearly giving the opening words of the codification. The table began:

If one summons another to court the latter must go. If he will not go, the plaintiff should proclaim the fact, then seize him. If he evades arrest or runs away, the plaintiff shall lay hands on him. If the person summoned is disabled through age or illness, the plaintiff shall provide a conveyance: he need not spread the carriage with cushions if he does not want to.

The Latin for this needs only thirty-four words. It is a model of brevity and attention to detail. The conclusion is inescapable that there was already a long tradition of draftsmanship at Rome.

3. Plautus, the comic playwright, who was born not later than 251 B.C. and died in 184 B.C., is the first Roman writer of whose work much has survived. He was keenly interested in law, and so his plays provide much useful information on the state of the law. Of course, one cannot rely on his accuracy, especially since his plays are adaptations of Greek models, but at the very least he often gives us the earliest indication of the existence of an institution.

Thus, in his *Captivi,* line 803, the parasite Ergasilus, who thinks he has made his fortune, declares:

I give notice in advance so that no-one may be caught on account of his own fault. Stay at home, keep away from the force of my violence.

As for the sow-keeping millers, who feed their pigs on swill, whose smell is such that no-one can go past the mill; if I see a sow of any of them on the public highway I will force the stuffing out of the owners themselves with my fists.

Likewise he tells what he will do to fishmongers and butchers. As his first word, *edico,* makes clear, Ergasilus is here parodying the Edict of the curule aediles, the magistrates who had control over the streets and marketplaces. This is the first evidence of the existence of any such Edict.[3]

4. The last century of the Republic was the great period of the development of the praetor's Edict. One of the major advantages of the

2. *De legibus* 2.4.9.
3. The earliest evidence of the praetor's Edict is also in Plautus *Asinaria* 371.

edictal system was its flexibility. Each praetor at the beginning of his year of office issued an Edict in which he would take over only those of his predecessor's rules which seemed useful. Hence an individual edict might change its form several times before it was accepted as fully satisfactory.

Thus, in the Edict of 73 or 72 B.C., the interdict concerning armed violence (*interdictum de vi armata*) began like this:

From which place by your fraud, Marcus Tullius, Marcus Claudius or his household or his procurator has been cast out.[4]

The model form in the Edict would, of course, have used standard, fictional names for the parties. In 69 B.C. Cicero had to deal with the interdict in another speech. But now, piecing together the words interpreted in *pro Caecina,* it ran:

From which place, you or your household or your procurator cast him out by force with a crowd or with armed men, restore him thither.[5]

Later there were other changes, though the course of them cannot be traced, and Hadrian's stabilized Edict read:

From which place, you cast him out by force with a crowd or with armed men, or your household cast him out, restore him and those things which he then had thither.[6]

5. Likewise, during the later Republic the jurists allowed themselves flexibility of interpretation, and gave decisions according to their own ideas of what was right and proper.

It is reported that Servius gave a reply that a creditor who wished to take less than the full amount from the debtor and release him, could accomplish this by taking coins several times from him, returning them and receiving them back again: for instance if the creditor wishes to release the debtor for one hundred when he has received ten; thus when he has accepted ten, gives them back to the debtor, at once receives them again and finally holds on to them.[7]

This is very curious behavior on the part of the creditor and debtor. The sole explanation must be that the debtor has no more than ten. That is why he never gives more than ten at any one time and also why the

4. Cicero *Pro Tullio* 12.19.
5. 14.41–17.48.
6. Reconstructed from *Digest of Justinian* 43.16.3 (Ulpian *69 Ad edictum*).
7. *Digest of Justinian* 46.3.67 (Marcellus *13 Digestorum*).

creditor is willing to release him on receiving ten. But why does the debtor not simply hand over the ten and receive a formal release from the creditor? The answer to this is that a debtor who announced he could not pay or made an agreement with his creditor that he could not pay the full amount of the debt suffered technical legal disgrace. The creditor in this instance was prepared to help his insolvent debtor to make it appear that he could pay and hence avoid the disgrace. And the jurist Servius was ready to accept the dodge as involving full payment.

6. The first two and a half centuries of the Empire are known as the classical period of Roman law because of the law's balance and maturity. One development during this period was the introduction of courses of legal study, and this led to the publication of students' elementary text-books, of which the most famous is Gaius's *Institutes.* These textbooks dictated substance as well as form and led to greater classification and organization of material. Much of our knowledge of legal abstractions derives from them. Thus, Gaius's *Institutes* begin:

Every people which is ruled by statutes and customs uses in part its own law, in part the law common to all mankind. For what each people lays down as law for itself is peculiar to it and is called the civil law *(ius civile)* as being the law peculiar to that State *(civitas).* But what natural reason has established among all men is observed everywhere and is called the law of nations *(ius gentium)* as being the law which all nations *(gentes)* use.

7. The great commentaries of the major jurists of the period–the commentary of Ulpian on the Edict was in eighty-three books–permitted not only detailed discussion of individual problems as we have seen, but also systematic treatment of the main principles. Here is the beginning of Ulpian's account (from his twenty-eighth book on Sabinus) of agreement in the contract of sale:

It is obvious that there must be agreement in contracts of sale: if there is disagreement about the fact of a sale or in the price or in anything else the sale is not perfect. Therefore if I thought I was buying the Cornelian estate, and you thought you were selling me the Sempronian estate, since we were not in agreement as to the object sold, the sale is void. The same is true if I thought I were buying Stichus, you thought you were selling Pamphilus, and the slave was not in our presence: for since there is disagreement as to the object it is clear there is no sale. 1. Of course, if we disagree as to the name of a thing but are in agreement as to the thing itself, there is no doubt that the sale is valid: for mistake as to name is irrelevant when there is agreement as to the thing. 2. Hence the question arises if there is sale if there is no mistake as to the thing, but there is mistake as to its substance, for instance if vinegar is sold as wine, bronze as gold or lead as silver, or anything else like silver as silver. Marcellus wrote in the sixth book of his Digest that there is sale because there is agreement as to the thing even though there is mistake as to its material. I agree in the case of the wine since the essence *(ousia)* is almost the same, provided it is wine gone sour. But if wine did not turn sour, but the vinegar was specially prepared vinegar from the start, one thing seems to have been sold as another. In the remaining cases, however, I think the sale is void whenever there is mistake as to the material.[8]

8. The drop in legal standards after the death of Ulpian is clearly reflected in the sources, in the constitutions emanating from the imperial chancellery as well as in the writings of individual jurists. A constitution of the Emperor Constantine of the year 319 A.D., which is preserved in the *Codex Theodosianus,* runs:

Thus it is settled that property descending from mothers is in the power of the fathers to the extent that they have ownership of possession, but they do not have the right and privilege of transferring it.[9]

In classical law ownership and possession were clearly distinct concepts, and the confusion of "ownership of possession" would have been impossible. In fact the right given to fathers by the constitution is closely akin to usufruct.

9. Justinian's contribution to legal science was not confined to codification. He also issued constitutions reforming the law. These display a new pomposity of language, which reflects the dignity he attributed to law.

In respect of things offered for sale, if a person bought a thing on the understanding that it was sold for the amount at which Titius valued it, a great doubt arose among many cultivators of the ancient wisdom. 1. To settle which, we ordain. . . .[10]

8. *Digest of Justinian* 18.19 pr.
9. 8.18.2.
10. *Code of Justinian* 4.38.15.

BIBLIOGRAPHY

SELECTED GENERAL WORKS
IN ENGLISH

A. TEXTBOOKS OF ROMAN LAW

Buckland, W. W. *A Textbook of Roman Law.* 3d ed. by P. Stein. Cambridge, 1963. The fullest and best modern textbook.

Buckland, W. W., and McNair, A. D. *Roman Law and Common Law.* 2d ed. by F. H. Lawson. Cambridge, 1952. A comparison in outline of Roman law and English law.

Lee, R. W. *The Elements of Roman Law.* 4th ed. London, 1956. A very satisfactory simple textbook which contains a translation of Justinian's *Institutes.*

Nicholas, B. *An Introduction to Roman Law.* Oxford, 1962. A good elementary textbook with references to modern civil law.

Schulz, F. *Classical Roman Law.* Oxford, 1951. A brilliant and very readable account of the law of the first 250 years of the Roman Empire by a scholar of rather extreme views.

Watson, A. *The Law of Obligations in the Later Roman Republic.* Oxford, 1965.

———. *The Law of Persons in the Later Roman Republic.* Oxford, 1967.

———. *The Law of Property in the Later Roman Republic.* Oxford, 1968.

———. *The Law of Succession in the Later Roman Republic* (to be published in 1970). Together these volumes attempt to examine every text which throws light on private law in the last two centuries of the Republic. Difficult reading.

———. *Roman Private Law around 200 B.C.* Edinburgh, 1970. A detailed account of the law of this early period.

B. HISTORIES OF ROMAN LAW

Jolowicz, H. F. *Historical Introduction to the Study of Roman Law.* 2d ed. Cambridge, 1954. [A third edition is being prepared by B. Nicholas]. A very readable account of the historical development both of substantive law and of the lawmaking organs.

Kunkel, W. *An Introduction to Roman Legal and Constitutional History.* Translated by J. M. Kelly. Oxford, 1966. Well-written account of the development of the Roman constitution and of sources of law.

Wolff, H.- J. *Roman Law: An Historical Introduction.* Norman, 1951. Simple account of the history of the sources. A long chapter deals with post-Roman developments.

C. TRANSLATIONS OF SOURCES AND COMMENTARIES

Johnson, A. C., et al. *Ancient Roman Statutes.* Austin, 1961. Translation of, and commentary on, pre-Justinianic statutes.

Jolowicz, H. F. *Digest XLVII.2; De Furtis.* Cambridge, 1940. Latin text, translation, and commentary on the *Digest* title on theft, with long and helpful introduction.

Lawson, F. H. *Negligence in the Civil Law.* Oxford, 1950. Latin text, translation, and commentary on the *Digest* title on the *lex Aquilia*, and other Roman and modern civil law texts. Useful introduction.

Moyle, J. B. *Imperatoris Iustiniani Institutionum libri quattuor.* 5th ed. Oxford, 1912. Latin text with commentary.

_____. *The Institutes of Justinian.* 5th ed. Oxford, 1912. A translation.

Oliver, D. T. *Digest XII.1 and 4-7, and XIII. 1-3, De condictionibus.* Cambridge, 1937. Latin text, translation, and short unhelpful commentary on the *Digest* titles on *condictiones.*

Pharr, C. *The Theodosian Code and Novels, and the Sirmondian Constitutions.* Princeton, 1952. Translation and commentary.

De Zulueta, F. *The Institutes of Gaius.* 2 vols. Oxford, 1946-53. Part 1 contains the Latin text with a translation, part 2 is a commentary.

_____. *The Roman Law of Sale.* Oxford, 1945. Selection of texts in Latin and translation, with the Sale of Goods Act 1893, Uniform Sales Act, and other modern statutes. Introduction.

_____. *Digest 41.1 and 2.* Oxford, 1950. *Digest* titles on acquisition of ownership and possession in Latin, with translation and commentary.

D. OTHER BOOKS

Crook, J. A. *Law and Life of Rome.* Ithaca, 1967. Law in its social setting. Lively book, but with a few surprising misunderstandings.

Daube, D. *Forms of Roman Legislation*. Oxford, 1956. Masterly insight into the "setting in life" of Roman enactments from the wording adopted.

_____. *Roman Law: Linguistic, Social, and Philosophical Aspects*. Edinburgh, 1969. Brilliant lectures delivered before the Faculty of Classics at Cambridge.

Honoré, A. M. *Gaius: A Biography*. Oxford, 1962. Ingenious reconstruction—mainly from very indirect evidence—of the life of the jurist Gaius.

Kelly, J. M. *Roman Litigation*. Oxford, 1966. A look at the social and political realities which conditioned litigation.

Lawson, F. H. *The Roman Law Reader*. Dobbs Ferry, N.Y., 1969. A selection of Roman legal texts and of writings on Roman law.

Schulz, F. *Principles of Roman Law*. Translated by M. Wolff. Oxford, 1936. Deals not with the rules of Roman law, but with the underlying spirit.

_____. *History of Roman Legal Science*. Oxford, 1946. An account of the making, application, exposition, and transmission of the law.

Stein, P. *Fault in the Formation of Contract in Roman Law and Scots Law*. Edinburgh, 1958. Detailed account. By far the greater part of the book concerns Roman law.

_____. *Regulae Iuris*. Edinburgh, 1966. Oversimple but smooth account of the development of legal maxims from Roman to more recent times.

Vinogradoff, P. *Roman Law in Mediaeval Europe*. 2d ed. Oxford, 1929, but recently reprinted in Germany. Brilliant short exposé.

Watson, A. *Contract of Mandate in Roman Law*. Oxford, 1961. Detailed analysis.

General Survey of Events, Sources, Persons, and Movements in Continental Legal History. By various European authors. London, 1912. Splendid chapters by specialist authors.

INDEX